# DESIGNED TO SUCCEED

# DESIGNED TO SUCCEED

a faith-driven blueprint to building the life you were created to live

Kevin Olusola and Donovan Dee Donnell
with Mark Tabb

ZONDERVAN BOOKS

*Designed to Succeed*


Published by Zondervan, 3950 Sparks Drive SE, Suite 101, Grand Rapids, MI 49546, USA. Zondervan is a registered trademark of The Zondervan Corporation, L.L.C., a wholly owned subsidiary of HarperCollins Christian Publishing, Inc.

Requests for information should be addressed to customercare@harpercollins.com.

Zondervan titles may be purchased in bulk for educational, business, fundraising, or sales promotional use. For information, please email SpecialMarkets@Zondervan.com.

ISBN 978-0-310-37014-7 (audio)

---

Library of Congress Cataloging-in-Publication Data

Names: Olusola, Kevin, 1988– author | Donnell, Donovan Dee, 1980– author | Tabb, Mark A. author
Title: Designed to succeed : a faith-driven blueprint to building the life you were created to live / Kevin Olusola and Donovan Dee Donnell with Mark Tabb.
Description: Grand Rapids, MI, USA : Zondervan Books, [2026]
Identifiers: LCCN 2026004201 | ISBN 9780310370123 hardcover | ISBN 9780310370130 ebook
Subjects: LCSH: Success—Religious aspects—Christianity
Classification: LCC BV4598.3 .O597 2026
LC record available at https://lccn.loc.gov/2026004201

---



HarperCollins Publishers, Macken House, 39/40 Mayor Street Upper, Dublin 1, D01 C9W8, Ireland (https://www.harpercollins.com)

*Cover design: Studio Gearbox*
*Cover photos: Ian Shiff / donbg photo designs*
*Interior design: Denise Froehlich*

***Printed in the United States of America***

26 27 28 29 30 LBC 5 4 3 2 1

# CONTENTS

# PROLOGUE

**KEVIN:** We should probably confess something before we go any farther. We didn't actually want to write this book.

**DONOVAN:** *At all.*

**KEVIN:** Not because we didn't think it was a good idea . . .

**DONOVAN:** . . . but because we were already doing a million things that felt important. And you know how sometimes God gives you an assignment and you're like, *I think you have the wrong number*?

**KEVIN:** Yeah, we tried to send him to voicemail. But the thing about God—he doesn't hang up.

**DONOVAN:** Instead, he signed us up for what I now call "purpose bootcamp." Late-night writing sessions. Honest conversations that made us sweat more than a Peloton ride. And moments of sitting in silence just waiting for direction like students in a class where the teacher refuses to give you the answer key.

**KEVIN:** And just when we thought we were writing *for you*, God was writing *in us*. Stretching us. Humbling us. Showing us where we still needed his touch before we could carry the next level of our calling.

**DONOVAN:** That's why we want you to read what follows with three intentions:

- Let each paradigm shift mess with you (the good kind of mess). Invite it in, position yourself in a growth mindset with prayer, and sincerely consider that idea.
- Find yourself in our stories, because you're in here somewhere. In one way or another the vulnerability of these stories will speak to you personally or connect with you through a relatable moment you've experienced or witnessed.
- Follow the practical tips at the end of each chapter. Highlighting this book isn't going to change your life the way you want. You can't "Amen!" your way into alignment. You have to apply what you read in it! Those practical tips at the end of each chapter? That's where the divine happens. That's where what you've read in black and white starts showing up in the color of your everyday life. Skip that part and this book just stays an inspiring treasure chest on paper. Do it and it becomes your personal playbook for experiencing success and walking in the life God has tailor-made for you.

**KEVIN:** And don't go it alone. Ask a friend to read it with you. That way, when you start dodging the hard stuff, your friend can text you, "Nah, come back. We're growing today."

**DONOVAN:** Our prayer is that by the last page, you'll believe that you were never designed to trade your soul for your dream. Success isn't about how to become someone else, it's about becoming more of who God made you to be. And when you develop yourself, align with his design, and multiply it all by faith, you'll realize you were designed to succeed. That includes everything you've been called to.

**KEVIN:** If he could get us—two very reluctant authors—to say yes to his idea of success, he can do the same with you.

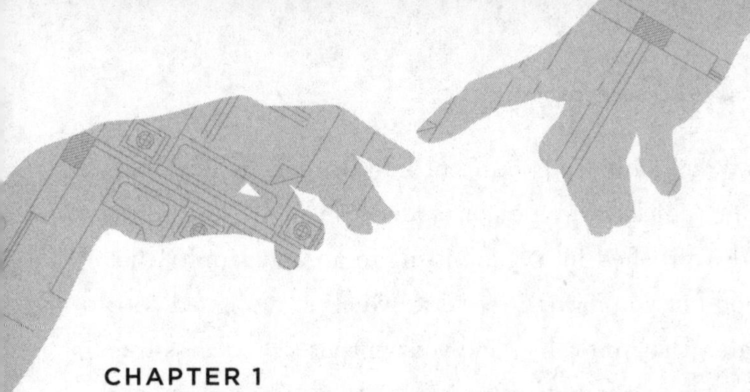

CHAPTER 1

# START WITH THE RIGHT QUESTION

Your first question going in is probably the most obvious: "If I'm designed to succeed, *how* do I do it?" You have dreams you're chasing and goals you're reaching for. It may be a business idea or an artistic itch or a calling to lead others. Whatever that something is for you, you feel deep in your bones that you must pursue it for your life to feel complete. You picked up this book maybe because you're looking for a list of habits to help you keep moving higher and farther, checking off one goal after another, making an impact, solving problems, reaching new levels of success consistently and efficiently so that you can create more success, add value, and influence your chosen arena. You want to learn the secret of reaching the next level. And the next. And the next. Because you want whatever is pushing itself out of you to grow and develop and take you to extraordinary places.

But asking how to get there is not the right question.

Asking how will only lead you right into the success trap: the life-draining, quicksand-type consequences you are left mired in after you've rushed into committing to an opportunity that looked good but you didn't first verify whether it aligned with who you are, what you value, and your purpose. A success trap looks like a big break, but instead of filling you, it drains your soul because it was never aligned with your God-given design. When you say yes to what glitters, you will find that it costs you your peace, health, and integrity.

True success is never a trap. Instead, it fulfills your purpose, realigns you, and fills you with the kind of lasting peace the world can't counterfeit.

Donovan and I have found through decades of pursuing success that the real starting point is not how but what: "What does success look like for me?" This goes beyond long- and short-term goals; it leads you to ask yourself, "Why these goals? Why this career path? What makes this record deal or this promotion or this relationship or this win so important that I am willing to pay the high price that success demands?" (And success always comes with a price!)

When you look beyond every outward measure of success, you are forced to ask yourself what you are really after. What will it take for you to call yourself successful? You may accomplish everything you ever set out to do, but how will you know whether you have done enough to satisfy that internal push that drives you to do the extraordinary? Until you wrestle with your definition of success, you will never know whether you have truly succeeded.

It's all too common to meet successful people who don't feel successful, usually because the only question they've ever asked is how.

Discovering how you are particularly designed to succeed starts by turning the mirror inward and getting honest about what success means to you individually, not just for today but for who you are becoming. Once you've answered the what, it will be time to ask whether that vision is big enough for an entire lifetime.

The truth is that goals shift. Seasons change. Pursuits evolve. But the kind of success that's rooted in who God designed you to be? That remains!

---

**KEVIN**

I know all too well the kind of success that fades even after reaching what I thought was the pinnacle. I was at the fifty-seventh annual Grammy Awards sitting near the front of the room at the Staples Center in Los Angeles shaking with nerves as Hilary Hahn started reading the list of nominees for the 2015 Grammy for Best Arrangement, Instrumental, or A Cappella. I glanced down the row at my Pentatonix bandmates. None of us could sit still. Sitting in that iconic venue on music's biggest night not as an observer but as a nominee, surrounded by all the legends in the industry, was the culmination of a lifelong dream. All my life I'd felt destined to do something great with my life, and Grammy night felt like mission accomplished.

I thought back four years earlier to when I made the risky decision to join the band. I had just graduated from Yale, having decided to turn my back on my lifelong goal of going to medical school for a career in music. Two weeks later, I became the beatboxer for a brand-new a cappella group. The five of us moved to Los Angeles and started rehearsing, looking for our distinctive sound. To make ends meet we shared a dingy apartment. Then came the first sign that we might be onto something big when we won the NBC talent show *The Sing-Off.* A month later we were back to square one after the record label dropped us because we weren't mainstream enough. *Maybe the label exec who made that decision is here tonight*, I thought. *If he is, I wonder what he's thinking now.*

Our category was one of those awarded before the live broadcast started, which meant we didn't have to wait all night to know whether we had won. I don't think I could have made it to the end of the night. When we got the news that we'd been nominated, my bandmates and I went from overjoyed (*I can't believe it!*) to shocked (*Is this really happening?*) to Christmas-morning excited (*Oh my gosh! Do you think we might actually win?*) in less than a second, and we kept riding that emotional roller coaster for the next three months. Everyone says it's an honor just to be nominated, and it was and still is, but deep down everyone who says that still wants to win. I know I did. I wanted it more than I ever imagined.

When I told my family and friends I was going to skip out on medical school to pursue a career in music, I felt guilty. Even if no one said it out loud, I could imagine their judgment: *So you're going to throw away a guaranteed future as a doctor with the money and prestige for* music? *Really? And you're going to do what? Beatbox? Isn't that the same thing as the noises you made when you were young that drove your dad crazy? That's your new career path?* But now I was part of a group nominated for music's most prestigious award!

Hilary read the last nominee's name. She paused a moment to tear open the envelope. My heart raced. Time stood still. Then Hilary glanced at the card, looked up, and said nine words I could not believe I was hearing: "And the Grammy goes to Pentatonix for 'Daft Punk.'" I locked eyes with my bandmate Scott Hoying. The two of us broke out in huge grins and both mouthed our very eloquent reaction to winning one of the highest honors the music industry can bestow: "Whoa!"

What came next was a blur. We went up onstage to receive our award, then it was backstage for interviews and then out for celebrations and everything else that told us we had reached the top. We'd gone from a canceled record deal to a Grammy in less than three years. *Surreal* can't begin to describe what I felt. Elated. Overjoyed. Overwhelmingly grateful. Satisfied. Validated. Vindicated. Successful. And just plain old happy. I could barely sleep that night. How could life get better than that?

The next morning the sun came up, and it was a brand-new, regular old day, which was followed by another brand-new, regular old day, and another and another until the thrill of my greatest accomplishment evaporated under the grind of the everyday. Only now the grind came with much greater pressure. Before "Daft Punk" we could fly under the radar. We were a band just trying to make it big. No one expected anything out of us but us. Not anymore. "Daft Punk" was a huge hit. In one year, our YouTube subscribers jumped from four hundred thousand to more than four million, and the "Daft Punk" video alone scored ten million hits in its first week. Now what were we going to do for an encore?

All we had accomplished so far was great, but every musician knows that people judge you by your latest performance. How were we ever going to top what we had just done? Was one Grammy enough? How would my bandmates and I handle it if we had already hit our peak as a band? Our album *That's Christmas to Me* had already gone platinum on its way to double platinum. But it was a Christmas album. People love Christmas albums. Our next album was all original music, about half of which I had a hand in writing. This new album was going to be a massive departure from our previous formula for success, in which we covered already popular songs. How were our fans going to react to the change? I had no idea. All I knew to do was to keep doing what had brought us this far: Keep working. Keep grinding. Keep pressing. Keep proving myself. That's the stuff of success and greatness—right?

A few weeks later I was onstage with the band performing "Daft Punk" on our On My Way Home tour. From the moment Mitch Grassi sang the first line, "Buy it, use it, break it, fix it," the crowd went absolutely wild. I did my beatboxing part like I did every night, but this performance felt different. As I sang, I had an out-of-body experience, as though I were standing off to the side watching myself, the crowd, and my bandmates. I saw myself going through the motions, but all I could think was, *Is this what success is supposed to feel like?* Standing on that stage three and a half months into our seven-month tour, I was living the dream. So why did it feel more like a chore than a joy?

The dictionary defines *success* as "the accomplishment of an aim or purpose; the attainment of fame, wealth, or social status."[1] By that definition, I'd attained it all. Mission accomplished. Why, then, did I feel so empty? Was this going to be my life now, just chasing the highs of awards and applause? Was I really going to let fame hijack my understanding of who I was? Was I lied to, or was I lying to myself the whole time? I didn't have the answers. But I knew I had to rethink and refashion success for myself, because what I was experiencing was not enough to satisfy that drive still bubbling up inside me.

**DONOVAN**

International bestselling author and speaker Dr. Miles Monroe once said that a man is drawn to praise.[2] I really resonate with his words because for much of my life I equated praise with success. I was conditioned by culture, movies, cartoons, family, and school to believe that succeeding in life was imperative. My hunger for success clothed as praise led me to a career choice I never thought I'd make: male exotic dancer—or fantasy salesman, as I often said.

Let's take a trip down memory lane. I was nineteen years old, and I didn't have anything very praiseworthy in my life at the time. I had just finished my first year at Morehouse College in Atlanta and had no desire to go back. I hadn't exactly flunked out, but my grades weren't great, and my heart was so broken by a relationship that had ended that moving back to LA with absolutely no idea what I was going to do next seemed like a better option than staying in Atlanta for my sophomore year. I'd always wanted to become an actor, but I'd struck out on almost every audition I'd gone to. Although my major in college was computer science, my fallback plan if acting didn't work out was modeling. I'd had some success with it in Atlanta, but not enough for me to stay there. At least that's what my nineteen-year-old brain kept telling me. At that time I was working at a fast-food restaurant for minimum wage, which wasn't enough to finance my basic needs and the extravagant dating experiences I desired to take my prospects on. Add to that, I was on academic probation for the first time in my life. I was fed up. I'd had enough of Atlanta. I was ready to go home to LA.

Not long after arriving back home to my old neighborhood, I ran into a friend from high school. While we were catching up, she mentioned she was dating a male exotic dancer. "You need to meet him," she told me. "I remember the way your shirt came off in every single pep rally in high school and how you danced around to get the whole school worked up. You'd be a natural."

If we'd had that conversation a year earlier, I probably would have laughed and said something about how I had bigger dreams for myself. But now with no better prospects, I said, "Okay. I'll meet with him." A day or two later I found myself at a club off infamous Crenshaw Boulevard with my friend and her exotic-dancer boyfriend. I told myself I was just going to check things out. But besides my friend, her boyfriend, and me, another presence was there: my bruised ego. And it needed a win.

I was hired on the spot. By the end of the night, I was

onstage dancing, 95 percent exposed, and doing what I believed I did best: enticing the crowd. I knew I could grab their attention and keep all eyes on me. More than that, I loved the high of being showered with praise using nothing but my looks and my body to get it. What I didn't know was the enormous influence that door I had just opened would have over my ability to resist succumbence in the next season of my life.

Despite growing up in church where my grandfather was the founder and pastor and still involved in Wednesday-night Bible studies, I kept going back to that stage night after night. For the next five years I worked up the most enticing dance routines that prompted the audience to give not only all the money they could but all their praise as well. And that praise became my addiction to the point that I traded personal safety and my mental health for it.

Now, here's the crazy part. When I was young, my mother taught me the importance of tithing, and even though I hoped my grandfather would never find out what I was doing for a living, every Sunday morning I stuffed an offering envelope full of dollar bills I'd made the night before and dropped it in the collection basket. Dancing made me a whole lot of money, and giving some away always made me happy. No one ever asked where the money came from, even though I'm sure they were curious. I think they were so grateful for my generosity that they decided to turn a blind eye to all the glitter on the bills. Giving stripper money to a church may seem blasphemous, but at the time I didn't want to see it that way. Instead, I just told myself it was an opportunity to contribute to my grandfather's ministry.

I felt very successful as a dancer, and by every measure I

was, but only because I forced myself to ignore my authentic self screaming from the basement of my subconscious:

*This isn't who you are!*
*The applause you hear isn't the approval you need.*
*You were made for more than the version of yourself they pay to see.*
*Your gift is influence, not seduction.*
*You can light up a room without dimming your soul.*
*Why do you feel empty after the lights go out?*
*This high fades too fast to be real joy.*
*You know the prayers your grandmother prayed over you. Does this look like the answer?*
*You were born to set people free, not bind them to fantasies.*

That was a lot to ignore. After a while I couldn't. I knew how to elicit the desired response from my audience. But it was all smoke and mirrors. My performance on the stage was just that, a performance. I had a look and a persona that I had created through working out at the gym, dyeing my hair, and changing my eye color with contact lenses. Yet the persona did not reflect who I was or communicate the message bubbling up inside me. Every compromise cracked open a little more of my soul that my authentic self was shouting through. Every quiet moment, every empty ride home, every time the music stopped, I'd hear that voice saying, *This isn't you. This isn't it. This isn't home.* God will let you feel the weight of a crown you were never meant to wear so that you'll crave the one he designed for you.

All my life I've found so much joy in sitting and reflecting, allowing my imagination to take flight as I explore my thoughts about what it means to be fully human. My exploration has led me to seek to connect with people on a deeper level. When I was a dancer, no one cared what was inside me. I had to keep my real self buried until I felt it start to slowly disappear.

As the years of dancing dragged on, I could not escape the sense that I was trying to win a race that wasn't meant for me. I knew *how* to succeed. The problem was, my what was all wrong. By chasing applause and praise, I had allowed myself to embody someone I was not. As a result, I could no longer consistently hold on to what mattered to me. I had defined success in a way that left me completely dependent on the reactions of others to my actions, rather than on my actions themselves. Cheers and applause and praise felt good, but what did any of it have to do with me? The cheers always faded. The applause always stopped. And the praise was always temporary. In the end, none of it really had anything to do with me. Yet that's where my definition of success had to begin: with me.

Ontology says that doing flows from being. We are before we do. Who, then, was I becoming as I chased what I wanted to achieve? Was I creating from who I already was, or from who I was pretending to be to accommodate the desires and fantasies of those around me? Philosophy whispers that virtue precedes achievement. Was my soul steady enough to hold the weight of the wins I hoped to attain in the material world?

Scripture makes it plain: A "good tree bears good fruit" (Matt. 7:16–17). What did the fruit of my life reveal about the roots I'd been growing and the idea of success I'd been chasing? And before I even started chasing the world's trophies, had I defined success for myself in alignment with the design God was already authoring in me?

These are the questions my soul pleaded with me to consider while also offering me a warning: If I didn't take time to wrestle with those questions, I might climb a ladder my whole life only to realize it was leaning on the wrong wall.

---

**KEVIN AND DONOVAN**

This may seem odd coming from a couple of guys writing a book on success, but here's the deal: We are not here to tell you what success should look like for you. That's a question you have to figure out for yourself. We are here to warn you that if your definition of success comes down to what you can accomplish or what you can acquire or how deeply you can impress others, that inner feeling of satisfaction that comes from reaching a goal or accomplishing something difficult will always be fleeting. Instead, our goal in writing this book is to show you a success that—instead of bouncing up and down between peaks and valleys—is sustainable on a daily basis with a more consistent upward trajectory.

Our search for true, lasting success led us to seek a success that transcends temporary accomplishments and is so complete that its residual benefit is passed down through generations. We want a constant—something that lasts, something that remains, something that leaves a legacy.

With such lofty goals, you may think we must have come

up with a very complex, esoteric, philosophical definition of success. We haven't. The definition of success we offer within these pages is actually very simple. To the dictionary's definition of success—"the accomplishment of an aim or purpose"—we add "while enjoying who I am made to be and doing what I am designed to do." With this definition we contend that real success is found not only in the goal reached but also in the satisfaction that comes from knowing that today I successfully pursued my life's purpose while staying true to myself.

It is through looking at the life of Jesus as revealed in the Bible that we arrived at our definition of success. Jesus did not measure his success by crowd size or popularity. He certainly didn't measure it by earthly possessions, since he basically didn't have any. Yet each day, he went out and did what he needed to accomplish for that day and that day alone. He was never in a hurry. He never got stressed about deadlines. Even with all he had to accomplish, Jesus always had time to get alone with the Father, hear his voice, and let his Father set his agenda for that day. Jesus shows us that success isn't about possessions or popularity but about daily alignment with the Father's voice, letting him set the pace and the plan for any and every accomplishment. That's the trajectory we are looking for!

We are convinced that a relationship with the God who made each one of us is the foundation that everything else in our lives builds upon. We believe that pursuing faith in God—a God who is not distant or hard to find but who made himself known personally through his Son, Jesus—is the key to unlocking all we've been called to be.

Several convictions undergird our understanding of success.

*First, we believe success has to be about more than what we do.* Achievements cannot define us. I, Kevin, am a musician and an artist, but I'm also a husband and a father. And now, through this book, I'm also a writer who gets to bring this message to life with one of my closest friends. Each of these roles individually reflects a portion of who I am, but no single one defines all of me.

*Second, the process of pursuing success should be enjoyable.* Read that again. Pursuing success should be enjoyable. That enjoyment begins with knowing, embracing, and enjoying your authentic self, the person you were created to be. That's important to understand, specifically because *created* implies a Creator who we believe has specifically and intricately designed us to fulfill a specific purpose.

*Third, real success comes only when we seek it as our authentic selves.* Too often, we live like imposters, performing roles and chasing goals that were never meant for us. The key is learning to spot when we're out of alignment so we can get back to living fully as the people God designed us to be. You'll need to be a critical thinker, something Donovan and I both try to be whenever we're faced with something new we need to consider and possibly lean in to.

I, Donovan, know all too well that in the race to get ahead and accomplish something remarkable, the pressure to give up authenticity for a costume is immense. I gave you a brief glimpse into my struggle with becoming who I thought I needed to be to acquire praise and affirmation. For five years I fought against myself, lying to myself and trying to believe that my false persona was just another side of me. It wasn't. And yet it took a string of experiences that you'll read about throughout this book before I could release that false narrative.

If you're wired to achieve, here's the reality: You will face the temptation to surrender parts of yourself in pursuit of your goals. It might look like cutting corners on an assignment to keep up your GPA; saying yes to everything so your résumé looks good; or letting your identity be defined by internships and LinkedIn titles instead of who you really are. It might be taking a promotion that demands so much of your time you start missing your kids' games, or slowly compromising your values to hit numbers, close deals, or stay ahead of competition.

On our podcast, *Imagine Faith Talk*, the two of us talk about this tension and how ambition without alignment can become the very thing that derails you. We've seen it: people sacrificing friendships, health, and faith for milestones they thought would make them whole, only to feel empty when they finally acquired them. The truth? If work becomes your driving factor when you know it should be your purpose from God that drives you, you'll burn out or sell out. You have to stay anchored in your values and your faith so the success you chase doesn't cost you the life you want to live.

Another common hindrance to real success is the internal battle with self-doubt. When I, Kevin, first joined a group of professional singers who had spent their entire lives training and developing their already massive talent for a shot at making it, believe me when I say I was filled with self-doubt. I was already a musician and had studied cello, saxophone, and piano, but I went to Yale and majored in East Asian studies while fulfilling my pre-med requirements. I had no idea how my background—which was so different from those of my bandmates—could work in our group. I felt pressured to become more like them. But I soon learned how my unique background and my differences became an asset for the group that contributed to our collective success.

As we wrote at the beginning of this chapter, the journey toward discovering how you are designed to succeed begins with asking the right questions: What does success look like to you? How do you define it? These are not rhetorical questions. Because we are addressing some of the basic ideas driven and successful people have about themselves, their work, and their lives, reading this book needs to be a reflective journey. We're going to ask a lot of questions that are meant to make you look deep within yourself and aid you in a type of self-discovery that will offer you clarity. And yes, these questions will be challenging, starting with maybe the most difficult of all: Who are you apart from your accomplishments?

You could skip this part. No one is hovering over your shoulder making you wrestle with who you are or where you are right now. You could just jump to the practical habits—the ones that help you "win"—without ever confronting what real success means. But here's the truth we've seen over and over again: If you bypass these questions, you risk trading long-term joy for short-term achievement.

We're not talking about adding more pressure to your life; we're talking about setting your life on a trajectory that will give you sustainable, God-centered joy in the middle of your journey. To set yourself in the right mindset, answer these questions: Who are the three most successful people you know? How do you know they are successful? What about them inspires you? What would they say is the key to success?

Please keep these three people in mind as you read the rest of this book. These references will help you understand how and why you see and feel success the way you do and how you define it for yourself.

CHAPTER 2

# UNDERSTAND WHO YOU ARE

At least five hundred years before Jesus' birth, at the Greek site of Delphi, on a mountain slope a few miles from the Gulf of Corinth, sat the temple of Apollo. Inscribed on one of the marble walls inside the temple were perhaps the two most quoted words from the ancient world: Γνῶθι σεαυτόν, "Know thyself." Or as Clint Eastwood's Dirty Harry says in the movie *Magnum Force*, "A man's got to know his limitations." The phrase is attributed to the Seven Sages of Greece, but Plato gave it the philosophical push that still rings true today. To Plato, to know yourself meant knowing your inner soul. Knowing who you are at your basic and authentic level.

True success is impossible without heeding Plato's advice. You have to understand who you are on the inside, apart from what you do or what others may think of you. You're probably asking, "How do I make that discovery?" In our experience, the most effective route comes through wrestling with three basic questions.

*What is most important to me?* What do I value? Whatever you value most defines success for you. No matter how many goals you reach or milestones you check off your list, if you do not consistently lay hold of that which you value most, you will not feel that deep satisfaction success can bring.

*What am I capable of doing?* This question is about more than your natural talents or refined abilities. Rather, the question is designed to go beyond abilities to capabilities, to go beyond talent to character. Asking this question requires pushing yourself to your limit until your limit backs up, which is the line where you learn a little more about who you are and what's within.

*What must I accomplish for my life to feel complete?* At first glance this question may seem to run counter to the goal of this chapter, as if our accomplishments define us. But this question is not about what goals you have set for yourself. Instead, it asks, What is your purpose for being? Why do you believe you are here? What is the ultimate reason for your life?

Before we dive into these questions, we offer a couple of words of caution. First, there is no shortage of people who would love to answer these questions for you. Whether it's someone you count as an authority in your life or those who applaud the loudest when you perform or those you hope will accept you into their group, we all face the temptation of allowing others to tell us who we are. Even worse is when we allow our insecurities and weak desires to define us. Ecclesiastes 4:4 tells us that most people are motivated to succeed because they envy their neighbors. We see someone who has what we want and we go out and remake ourselves to fit what it will take to have what they have. As the ancient teacher concluded, this is meaningless, like chasing after the wind.

Second, the questions we offer are best answered under a certain type of pressure; otherwise, all you will find are your ideals, not reality. When life is easy, these questions are even easier. What do you value? *Love. Relationships. Family. God.* What are you capable of doing? *Anything I set my mind to.* What must you accomplish for your life to be complete? *Something that leaves a legacy that will inspire my kids and grandkids and their kids.* Like we said, this exercise is easy—until life goes a little sideways. Then what we claim we value on our best day means little on our worst. When who I am on my worst days outmuscles who I want to be on my best, life slips out of alignment. This chapter and the two that follow are designed to help us get in or get back into alignment, with both how we want to be and who we were designed to be. We have found this to be a liberating process as well as a crucial first step toward success that gets us off the roller coaster of chasing goals.

Again, like all the other questions in this book, the following discovery questions will take you only as deep as you allow yourself to go. The more honest you are with yourself, the more efficiently and effectively you will move from a feeling of frustration even while succeeding to consistent satisfaction in whatever season you may find yourself—even if it doesn't look like success to anyone else!

Okay, let's dive in.

## Question 1: What Is Most Important to Me?

DONOVAN

Growing up in Los Angeles, I passionately wanted to be an actor, just like maybe every kid who grows up in the shadow of the Hollywood sign. After I moved back to LA and started dancing, I still hoped to break into acting. I took some classes at Van Mar Academy of Motion Picture and Television Acting, where they focused on making stars. That training took me emotionally and psychologically into spaces I hadn't visited within myself before. It was therapeutic and enlightening and fun. Later on I landed a part in an AT&T commercial. The commercial checked one box. It was an accomplishment, but in my soul it didn't feel like success. It was more of a résumé win than a life win.

Then one day my cousin and I were standing in line at McDonald's talking ambition, hopes, dreams, and girls when a man walked up to us and said, "I manage models and I like your look. Here's my card." This wasn't Hollywood knocking, but it felt close enough to dream.

A few days later, after a few phone conversations, I found myself in a Hollywood house for a photoshoot audition. Once the basic personality shots were out of the way, he handed me boxer briefs and told me to model them. I put them on, and we started shooting again. I thought it was going well until he stopped shooting and asked me if I could, well, arouse myself for the next shots. I felt like my spirit was being cornered. What he asked me to do didn't feel like part of the job. It felt as though he had just asked part of me to step away from who I really was. At the same time, I couldn't help but ask myself what the difference was between his request and what I had already done for hundreds of women at the strip club. I didn't have an answer, but one thing was clear: That moment didn't awaken my creativity, it tested my convictions.

I swallowed hard, heart pounding, and said, "I'm not sure how I feel about this."

He looked at me unfazed.

"I have a girlfriend and a relationship with God—" I started again.

But he cut me off. "Listen," he said, voice low and unflinching, "in this business, talking about God only hurts you. No one cares about your relationship with God or your girlfriend." Then his energy shifted as if an entirely different spirit took over, and he said with surprising sincerity, "I don't usually do this, but I'll give you a couple of days to think this over. You have the look. I could get you to New York Fashion Week. But to make it, to stay on top, you'll have to do what you have to do. You sleep with whoever you have to, cut corners if need be. The question is this: Are you willing?"

Two truths collided in my soul. On one level, I wanted that spotlight. My *doing* seemed ready. But my *being*—my values, my character, my faith—shouted, *Not this way!*

I took those couple of days to think and pray before I said no. I could have chased the ticket to fame. But I knew that even if I'd landed that modeling career, walked runways in New York, transitioned to acting, I'd be doing it alone. Empty. So I walked away, trying to calculate all that saying no had just cost me. I never booked that agent. I never modeled for New York Fashion Week. I never made the crossover into Hollywood stardom.

I've never regretted that moment, because deeper than modeling success was the success I found in belonging to a life where love, integrity, faith, and identity aren't negotiable. I wasn't living fully in that conviction at the time, but I was wrestling with it. And I wanted it to be completely true for me even though my life didn't reflect that conviction. When faced with such a stark choice, I realized that alignment with God's design wasn't just a philosophy. It was the only kind of success that wouldn't cost me myself.

Where is your line? If someone offered you your dream opportunity but it required you to compromise your values, would you recognize the moment and walk away? Or would you surrender what you said was important to chase what you wanted?

The line is not always so clearly defined. Rarely are we asked to surrender everything. Instead, we all face small, day-to-day, hour-to-hour, even minute-to-minute decisions in which our true priorities are revealed. Perhaps the best way to answer the question of what is most important is to ask a far more mundane question: What do you do day in and day out? How do you spend your time? Look past your daily schedule and take an honest look at what you actually do. What situations or activities or entertainment do you find yourself naturally gravitating toward? The answers to these questions reveal some uncomfortable truths. For instance, I can say relationships matter, but if I never invest any time in people, relationships aren't nearly as important to me as I claim.

Now think about your best self, your most successful self, the person you strive to be. Take a deep breath and answer:

- What is most important to this version of you?
- How does this version compare with what you see play out in your day-to-day life?
- When you imagine the highlight reel of your life, does it feature moments of compromise or moments of courage?
- If you stripped away every "should," every fear, and every external expectation, who would you be? What would you protect? And what would matter so deeply that without it every other form of success would feel empty?

Success begins with not only understanding what is most important to you but also aligning those values with your daily habits and practices and skills. As Kevin and I wrote earlier in the chapter, no one else can tell you what matters most to you. You have to decide for yourself.

### Question 2: What Am I Capable of Doing?

KEVIN

Pentatonix had our first taste of success early on when we won *The Sing-Off*. But a taste is not the same as the whole thing. Even after we won the show, the five of us continued to live in the same apartment complex in Los Angeles that wasn't exactly in the fanciest part of town. The promised record deal that came with our win had fallen through, which meant as a band we still had a lot of work to do to get to where we wanted. Yet none of us cared. Honestly, those were some of the best days of my life as the five of us developed our music and our sound. We arranged. We wrote. We recorded. We put together videos that we uploaded onto YouTube in search of our audience. It was great! I believed that God had called me to pursue music and I was as happy as humanly possible while I followed that call. What others saw as a struggle, my bandmates and I looked at as an adventure. We were a long way from everything the future held for us, but we were living the dream.

Then my dad flew out from Kentucky to visit me. He didn't say a lot while at the apartment, though I could tell by the look on his face that he had something to say. But he was holding back. Then, shortly after he left, my phone dinged. When I saw it was a text from my dad, I felt a little sick to my stomach. I felt even worse when I opened it and started reading. He wrote something like this: "Son, I love you, and I have sacrificed so much for you all of your life. Your mother and I came to this country and worked hard to get to where we are, and we made sacrifice after sacrifice for you. I took out loans against my practice to send you to the best schools in America. We did everything in our power to make it possible for you to have every advantage and every opportunity. And now this is the life you've chosen? I hope you reconsider!"

His words cut deep. As a child of immigrants who had lived out the American dream, I grew up idolizing my parents. My father was not exaggerating about the sacrifices he made for me and our family. His early childhood was spent in a small one-room mud house in Ibadan, Nigeria, with his four siblings. But he worked hard, came to the States, and went on to become one of the most respected psychiatrists in Owensboro, Kentucky. To get there he had to overcome all sorts of barriers, including blatant racism. My mother did as well. The two of them instilled in my siblings and me the same drive, the same sense of purpose and obligation. For as far back as I can remember, my mother always told me, whatever I did, to be "extraordinary and uncommon." Never take the easy road. Always push myself to be the best I can possibly be. And do something with my life that matters, that changes lives. Did trying to make it as a pop a cappella band measure up to that standard? My father certainly didn't think so. He and my mother always thought medicine was the best path, just as they had done. My mother was a nurse with a master's degree in public health. When my dad taught me to write my signature, he did a scribbled signature just like doctors do. I practiced it over and over again, but then I added the letters *MD* to the end to signify my future career. To me, it was an opportunity to honor the man whom I respected so much; to me, *MD* meant "my daddy."

But I also knew that my parents' plans for my life and their measures of success did not align with the ones I believed God had put right in front of me. I knew God had called me into music. I felt his divine hand guiding me, which is what made this entire episode that much more difficult. I felt torn between my love for my parents and my deep desire to please them, and the path I felt God had laid out for me. Even so, I knew which path I had to take.

I thought about my dad's text for a while before composing my reply. I told him, "Dad, I love you and Mom. I have never forgotten anything the two of you taught me. It's just that I believe God has called me to apply it to music, not medicine." I then added at the end, "If music does not work out, I can still take the MCAT and go to medical school."

The experience taught me something very important about my capabilities. I knew I had two sets of abilities, music and science, both of which I loved. When I completed all my pre-med requirements at Yale, the process wasn't drudgery. I enjoyed every moment of it and did well in my classes. Until God opened the door for me to pursue my passion for music, I could never imagine doing anything with my life other than becoming a doctor. So the question was not which of my abilities I needed to maximize. Honestly, when I chose music, I believed I chose the weaker of the two. Giving in to my dad, moving back to Kentucky from LA, and going to medical school was the easiest, maybe even the most logical choice. But by sticking to the path I believed God had laid out for me, I discovered I was capable of going my own way even at the risk of disappointing the two most important people in my life.

This is what we mean when we ask, What are you capable of doing? Yes, this question can make our imagination go nuts thinking about all we could do with our abilities and opportunities. But to pursue deeper, fuller success, your authentic self has to dig deeper and ask hard questions like these:

- Do I have the conviction to choose a path others question?
- Do I have the resilience to stick to a task when giving up would be easier?
- Do I have the persistence to keep working toward a goal when it takes longer to reach it than I had planned?

- Am I able to give up a goal—even after investing a great deal of time and resources, even though it would be embarrassing—when it becomes clear that giving it up is the only way to move forward with life?

As high performers, we know our abilities. We spend years refining them. Understanding our capabilities is the next step, one that opens the door to understanding ourselves.

A few years after that text conversation with my father, he sat next to me the night my bandmates and I won our second Grammy. Not only did we win a Grammy that night, but I had the privilege of singing with Stevie Wonder onstage and presenting Ed Sheeran his Grammy for Song of the Year. The night was nothing short of unbelievable. In the middle of it all, my dad leaned over to me and said, "Congratulations on your Grammy. . . . When are you going back to medical school?"

My heart dropped. I could not believe he asked me that. I looked over at him, incredulous, and said, "You have got to be kidding!"

My father threw back his head and laughed like I had never heard him laugh before. "Of course I am kidding. I am so proud of you, son. Congratulations." I never knew my dad was capable of getting me like that!

### Question 3: What Must I Accomplish for My Life to Feel Complete?

What would you do with your life if you didn't need to impress anyone? What would you do if you were free from the endless cycle of accumulating likes and comments and gaining followers? What if you didn't need applause, didn't need approval, didn't need acceptance? What would you do if you were free from every expectation, from all the pressure to live up to someone else's ideal about who you should be and what you should do? Where then would you invest your time and talents, your abilities and capabilities? If you could eliminate all the noise screaming at you telling you what you should do, what would you do? Who would you be? What would you point at and say, "This is why I am here, this is why I am alive, this is my reason for living"? Of all the questions we've asked, this may be the most difficult to answer.

---

**KEVIN**

Once Pentatonix hit our stride, life felt like a whirlwind of touring, concerts, recording sessions, even television specials. That whirlwind came to an abrupt halt in March 2020. All our tour dates were canceled for the foreseeable future. We couldn't get together in the studio to record because of the whole social-distancing and shelter-in-place dynamic. In one day I went from barely having time to think to having nothing but time to sit around in my own head. That can be dangerous for me because I tend to overthink. I knew I needed to stay out of that trap, so I began to spend a lot of time making solo music and digesting online content about high performance. I also sought out a high-performance coach.

During one of my early coaching sessions, Brian, my coach, asked me, "Kevin, why do you want to be successful?" I had an instant, easy answer about glorifying God that I was about to rattle off. But before I could get the words out, he hit me with a second question that rocked my world: "What's the scariest thing that could happen that you would count as failure?"

I didn't stop to think about my answer. I just blurted, "The number one thing I'm most scared of in my life is to be given all of these talents and for the world not to recognize them or see them in their totality."

"So you are trying to be successful to validate your existence? You just want to be liked," Brian said.

I sat there in shock. Brian was right, but I never saw what should have been right in front of my face. No matter how much I might have said otherwise, to be liked—an outcome I had no control over—was what I thought I needed for my life to feel complete. I could say that everything I did was to glorify God or provide for my family or any of the other standard answers, but those weren't my only reasons. I faced the very real possibility that they weren't my reasons at all.

Deep down I knew that Brian was right. Being liked was my top priority—how I answered the question of what success looked like for me—which pretty much guaranteed I would never find satisfaction at any level of success. No matter how loud the applause, I would always crave more. And more.

I hated to admit it, but I was living out the message of Ecclesiastes: "Everything is meaningless . . . completely meaningless" (1:2 NLT). The writer of Ecclesiastes goes on to ask what people get for all their hard work under the sun. No matter what we do, no matter how great an impact we think we have on the world, the world remains the same.

But that's not the worst of it. In verse 8 he writes, "Everything is wearisome beyond description. No matter how much we see, we are never satisfied. No matter how much we hear, we are not content" (NLT). And then he adds the kicker in verse 11: "We don't remember what happened in the past, and in future generations, no one will remember what we are doing now."

My experience has taught me that landing on an answer that goes deeper than the usual superficial expressions of success is only half the battle. God made us to enjoy a relationship with him and to reflect him in everything we do. My greatest priority is to glorify God. I believe that is the reason any of us are on this earth. Living it out does not come naturally, though. Putting that priority into practice requires daily, if not hourly or even minute-by-minute, course corrections to keep what I most want to accomplish front and center in my life. Like an old house that requires constant maintenance, we have to work to keep our focus not only where we need it to be but also where we most want it to be.

## Finding the Truest Version of Yourself

Most of us, when we explore what is most important to us along with what we are capable of doing and what we must do for our lives to feel complete, do not land on a single version of ourselves. We often bounce between who we want to be, who we are, and who we are in the process of becoming. Yet the different versions of ourselves are all still us. What changes are the ways we think, act, and carry ourselves based on our levels of growth, awareness, and alignment. Those "versions" aren't different identities. They are different expressions of the same soul, shaped by the choices we make, the truth we live, and our stage of personal and spiritual development.

So who are you at this moment? Who do you aspire to be? Who are you in the process of becoming? While you consider these questions, focus on these parts of yourself to understand how you are designed to succeed:

- Your aligned self: The version of you that lives in sync with God's will, not just your own ambition
- Your disciplined self: The version that makes choices based on long-term vision, not short-term feelings
- Your resilient self: The version that can stand in faith through storms, setbacks, and seasons of waiting
- Your true self: The version that stops performing for approval and starts living from your identity in Christ
- Your legacy self: The version that thinks beyond personal gain and invests in impact that will outlast you

The goal isn't to switch between versions but to cultivate a single version: the authentic, aligned, God-centered you that goes beyond accomplishments, beyond popularity, beyond material comfort to attaining your true purpose. Therein lies real joy, deep satisfaction, and sustainable peace.

CHAPTER 3

# EMBRACE YOUR UNIQUE DESIGN

KEVIN

One morning in February 2012, I opened up Twitter and saw that I'd received a direct message from Quincy Jones! I could not believe it. My heart started beating so fast I could barely open it. In the message Jones said, "I love your cello-boxing, I love 'Julie-O,' I love what you do. I'd like for you to come to my house so I can meet you." Football players dream of playing in the Super Bowl and baseball players dream of playing in the World Series, but for a young musician like me, this was bigger than either of those. *The* Quincy Jones had not only heard and liked my music, but he wanted to meet me. Two months later I found myself in Quincy Jones's Bel Air home, with my cello, playing "Julie-O" for him and his executive manager. We then hung out in his home theater watching and discussing videos of him working with some of the greatest legends in music, like Michael Jackson.

As if hanging out with Quincy Jones were not enough of an out-of-body experience, a couple of weeks later I received an invitation to open his part of the Montreux Jazz Festival in Switzerland. Of course I said yes. This was the biggest thing that had ever happened to me! And me being me, I immediately began overthinking it. Right before my performance I was so nervous I didn't know whether I could even go onstage. But then Quincy came over to me and said, "Bro, chill out. Calm down. Just be you. I asked you here because only you can do what you do." That was all I needed to hear. I went out and did what I do.

I wish I could say that from that moment forward I lived by Quincy's advice. It wasn't until after fifteen years of trying and failing and learning, and after I started working on my own solo album, that I finally understood what he was trying to say: Just be you. I was never going to succeed if I conformed to a "norm." I needed to stop competitively comparing myself with successful people. If I changed to be like them, I could never be me. I might hit some goals by imitating what I thought it took to be successful, but the accomplishment would be empty. Faux success is worse than no success. I had to explore my own giftedness. I needed to embrace my unique design. Real success comes only by chilling out, calming down, and being yourself.

## Shift Your Perspective

I always knew I was a musician. My parents knew it too. They saw the first signs when I was six months old as I clapped along with songs in perfect beat. When I was almost three years old, I played the Animals' "House of the Rising Sun" by ear on a small electric piano for my father. He immediately enrolled me in piano lessons. When I was six, I fell in love with cello when I was in a violin class that my sister, Candace, was taking with Dr. Mack, a cellist trained at the Eastman School of Music. At one point, she invited me to play, but I wasn't interested, nor did I actually know what a cello was. Later, she gave me a wooden box shaped like a cello without the strings and taught me some basic techniques, and then soon after she offered me a kid-sized cello to play. My mom and she both said, "Any time you want to stop, you can stop." But I was starting to enjoy playing, and I was progressing quickly in the strings class. When I started taking cello lessons, I never realized I was one of the only black kids in the studio. I just loved being around music. Then when I was ten, I started playing the saxophone and at twelve toured Europe as part of the United States Collegiate Wind Band. I made first-chair saxophone for the tour even though I was about to be an eighth grader in a band filled with high school students.

Though I loved music and my parents supported my musical pursuits, for the first twenty years of my life I never considered music as a possible career path. I was against it as much as my parents were. I remember a man coming up to me after a piano recital when I was in junior high and saying something like, "Kevin, that was great. You should really think about a career in music." He meant it as high praise. I took it to mean that since I was black, my options in life were limited, coming down to being either a musician or an athlete. I now know that he meant nothing of the kind, but in my teenage mind that's what I heard. I made it my goal to show that guy and everyone like him that no one was going to dictate my future based on the color of my skin. Instead, I planned to go into a field not necessarily stereotyped as a black space: medicine.

Since this chapter is called "Embrace Your Unique Design," you may expect me now to explain how medicine was my square peg in a round hole while music was the perfect fit. But that's not the truth. When I decided to pursue music instead of medicine, I actually took the path for which I was least qualified. Chemistry and biology and everything else I had to take to fulfill my pre-med requirements at Yale were things I knew I could work hard enough to pursue, and it helped that I enjoyed them as much as I did. Music was a nice hobby, but medicine saved lives—and that's what mattered most. At least that's what my immigrant parents instilled in me. They taught me that the greatest use of a life is to invest it in the lives of others in a way that leaves the world a little better than when you came into it. Obviously the best way to do that was to aim for one of the immigrant holy trinity of careers: doctor, lawyer, or engineer. Since my dad was a doctor and my mom a nurse, the choice was easy. I did not see my parents' expectations as a bad thing. Instead, I was glad they saw potential in me, and I wanted to make them proud.

So what changed? The easy answer would be me, although that's not completely true. I did not change, but the way I saw myself did. The funny thing is, that realization hit me while I was doing something unrelated to music while studying on the opposite side of the world. It all started with opening my mind to the possibility that what I had always considered normal didn't have to be.

### Let Your Uniqueness Define Your Normal

I spent the summer after my sophomore year of college studying abroad at the Harvard Beijing Academy in China. During one of my conversational Chinese classes, we had to share something about ourselves. When my turn came, I said something like, "I'm pre-med, but also an academic music major at Yale. My favorite instrument to play is the cello. Oh, and I also beatbox for fun," which was accompanied by a brief beatboxing sample. Of course, I said this in Chinese.

The professor, a Chinese national, sort of nodded along, and when I finished, he asked, "Have you ever thought about combining the two?"

"The cello and beatboxing?" I asked, more than a little surprised by his question.

"Yes," he said.

I shook my head, smiled, and said, "No." I could have added, "That's the craziest idea I've ever heard!" This professor obviously knew very little about classical music or beatboxing; otherwise, he never would have made such a crazy suggestion.

Or was it crazy?

After class I went back to my dorm room, but I could not stop thinking about his question: Had I ever thought about combining the two? I never had, but not because I thought it might be extremely difficult to do. Lots of people sing and play an instrument at the same time. Beatboxing while playing the cello should be no different. No, the reason why never in a million years would I have thought about combining the two was because they come from such different worlds with completely different sets of norms. I grew up taking cello lessons from classically trained teachers and also attended summer music programs taught by college professors. Not only did I learn the instrument, I also learned the world of classical music and the hundreds of years of pedagogy behind it. Beatboxing did not belong in that world. I mean, honestly, could anyone imagine Beethoven beatboxing?

And yet there was something about the absurdity of the idea that made me curious. I took out my cello and started messing around. I liked what I found. But a voice in my head kept telling me that every one of my cello instructors would hate it. Anyone who loved classical music would hate it.

Why, then, didn't I hate it?

And why did I care how some invisible group out there might react?

It helped that this conversation with myself happened more than seven thousand miles from Yale. The distance gave me the freedom to experiment until I had something worth sharing. Later that summer I introduced what I dubbed cello-boxing during one of the Harvard Beijing Academy's showcase nights with a performance of a simple hip-hop groove with cello chords that I created in my room. Afterward, my professor came up to me and asked, "Are you a ghost?" because he had never seen anything like that before.

When my study abroad program ended, I went back to Yale and

kept experimenting with cello-boxing. After my junior year, I took an academic year off to study higher-level Chinese at the Inter-University Program for Chinese Language Studies at Tsinghua University in Beijing and continued developing my gift. That summer living in Beijing, I attempted to work on my own version of Mark Summer's classical piece "Julie-O." Once I had something I felt worth sharing, I played "Julie-O" for my cello teacher that fall. He then had me play it for my cello studio class. Half the class thought it was sacrilegious, while the other half thought it was the coolest thing they'd ever heard. Now I had to decide which half I was going to listen to. The answer seemed pretty obvious. Long story short: In April of my senior year, a recording of me playing "Julie-O" ended up on YouTube and went viral. Three friends from Texas who were in the process of starting an a cappella group watched it. Afterward, Scott Hoying (and show producer Ben Bram) contacted me about joining him and his friends for an audition for an NBC talent show. That's how I ended up becoming a part of Pentatonix, all because, instead of following the norm for classical music, I let my unique abilities and personhood define normal for me. I never set out to change the norms for any space other than for myself. When I did, opportunities presented themselves that I never would have discovered any other way.

All of this unfolded over time, beginning with a shift in perspective that grew into a belief that clarified into a vision, which eventually grew into a new normal. Getting comfortable with not being comfortable allowed me to execute out of my design. I didn't set out to shift any paradigms or disrupt standards and norms. I didn't need to.

Embracing your unique design doesn't first change the world, it changes you. The door then opens for you to do things that others may have never thought of doing before. Will this new normal always be successful? No. In life, there are no guarantees, only opportunities, most of which you have to create for yourself. And you may fail at times in doing it. But that's exactly how you develop expertise!

Getting past preconceived ideas and norms is only the first step in embracing your unique design. There's another step that can be even harder: learning how to do something new when the skills are nonexistent. It certainly was for me. It wasn't just that I no longer fit into classic stereotypes. I could get past that. It was that years after I created cello-boxing, the desire to explore new facets of creativity was growing inside me again, but I didn't yet have the skills I needed. I was faced with a new challenge in discovering and embracing who I am: I was about to embark on something that felt downright impossible to attempt, and maybe downright stupid.

## Build on Your Differences Without Getting Stuck in the Trap of Comparison

In 2015 I released my first EP, which included my first original cello-boxing piece, "Renegade." The EP went to the top of both the classical and the classical crossover charts. To my surprise, one response I heard over and over was, "This is cool, but can you actually sing too?" Apparently beatboxing vocals were not enough. People needed words. A girl I was dating at the time also repeatedly brought up singing: "Kevin, why don't you take voice lessons and learn to sing?" I found the questions and suggestions annoying. For one thing, I had just released what I believed to be a very creative, very innovative album, especially for the cello. Was my solo EP somehow diminished because I did not sing on it? I didn't think so, but from what I heard from way too many people, I had somehow missed the mark.

The more people asked me about it, however, the more I started thinking seriously about the question. I already used my voice as an instrument. Could I train it to sing as well? I was content doing what I was doing for now, but what about in the future? Up to this point, I'd defined much of my life by exploring different aspects of my creativity and artistry. Was I ready to stop now? No! I also thought about one of my dad's favorite artists, George Benson. Benson started out as a jazz guitarist, but his career really took off when he started singing with his distinctive style. I started to see myself doing the same thing.

But there was still one thing that made me question my sanity for even thinking about working toward a solo project featuring my own vocals. I worked with some of the best singers in the world every single day. Compared with them, all I could make was noise. Musically, I felt like a kid drawing with crayons while my Pentatonix bandmates were painting masterpieces. I could not get past the question of how I could possibly do what they were doing. I could take voice lessons for the rest of my life and still not measure up.

And then I met Sting.

I happened to be backstage at the NBC Rockefeller Center Christmas tree lighting broadcast, on which both Sting and

Pentatonix were scheduled to appear. I knew he was there, but I was too intimidated to approach him on my own. But when my manager spoke to his manager about the chance to meet him, I jumped at the opportunity. I expected maybe a handshake and a quick hello, but Sting invited me to sit down and talk. When I asked him about how he developed his distinctive vocal style and musical art, he told me something along the lines of, "Kevin, I don't really sing like everyone else, but I know what my voice can do specifically for me. I also know the kinds of songs that work for me, not just for my voice but for the tapestry I want to paint with the song and production. Once I understood all of this, I started writing songs that made sense for me."

My hesitation gave way to excitement. I felt like Sting had kicked the door open for me. No, I will never sing like my band-mates do. But they will never sing like me, not if I focus on songs that work for my voice and my personality and my story. No one can. And that's the point. When we compare ourselves with others, all we can see are our deficiencies. But when we embrace our uniqueness and focus on developing what we already have, our eyes open to so many new possibilities. Instead of competing with others to try to become number one, we are free to follow God's call to be the only one.

My field is music, but the same principle works in whatever space you occupy. The process begins with acknowledging your differences instead of shrinking from them. Only then can you understand how your differences give you a perspective that others do not have. You will then see new possibilities or needs or even problems to avoid that others in your space cannot see or have never considered. Instead of trying to be exactly like your teammates, you can lean in to your specific skills, which makes you even more valuable to your team because it allows for deeper, fuller, richer collaboration. It's where the magic happens.

### Lean In to Your Areas of Struggle

No matter how many doors I saw open as I allowed my uniqueness to define my normal, and no matter how many times I reminded myself that God called me not to be the best one but to be the only one in my space, I still struggled with what Donovan and I have found to be one of the biggest barriers to embracing one's unique design: imposter syndrome. I did not think I was prepared enough. I did not feel like I was good enough. I did not feel like I had what it took to occupy the particular space I was in. Every day, I woke up half expecting someone to tell me, "The jig is up. It's time to leave."

Why did I feel like a fraud? Because it wasn't all easy! I struggled both to develop my singing voice and to produce the desired result. There are days even now when I feel the same way. I also struggled to come up with lyrics for my original music. Nothing flowed. Every song felt like a battle with myself. Compared with my bandmates, my singing voice felt weak. The more I struggled, the more I asked myself, "How can I belong in this space if staying here is so difficult?" I believed that God knew this environment was best for me, but that knowledge alone didn't make the imposter syndrome go away.

DONOVAN

When I coach people who are struggling with imposter syndrome, I often remind them that even though the first manned spaceflight took place in August 1961 and hundreds of people have traveled *through* space since then, no one has ever gone *into* space. People have walked on the moon, but no one will ever do it barefoot. Neil Armstrong, the first man on the moon, did not scoop up a handful of moon dust and let it run through his bare fingers, like a child playing with sand on a beach. He and Buzz Aldrin did not pack swimsuits for sunbathing outside the lunar module. Astronauts survive by enveloping themselves in space suits—earth bubbles, if you will—that protect them from an environment for which human bodies were not made. Even a pinprick in the bubble is fatal.

Many of us convince ourselves the same will happen if we reveal aspects of our authentic selves, especially those areas we deem weaknesses. A space suit I often put on as I stepped into the profession of a life coach was dressing in a way that made me look less threatening. I saw my features as a weakness compared with how others looked who were doing what I wanted to do. Like Kevin, we too often label any place where we struggle as a weakness. So we believe we have to become masters of disguise to cover up our real selves, which struggle to do what comes easily to others within the space we want to occupy. That disguise is our space suit, the comfortable bubble we wrap ourselves in so we can enter or remain in places we've convinced ourselves we do not truly belong. We justify our disguise with sayings such as "Fake it till you make it," when really what we are saying is

"I cannot do this as me. I have to become someone else to stay here." As a result, we often sacrifice our integrity or the people we love. Yet any success we may achieve in the disguise never gives that deep sense of inner satisfaction we crave, because it's counterfeit.

Rather than camouflage the struggles, I encourage my clients to recognize them for what they are: a necessary step to the next level of growth. Within our areas of struggle we discover things about ourselves we cannot learn any other way. Invariably, these truths we unearth are the missing pieces we need to continue moving upward. If we never struggle, we will never discover what we are capable of doing. I've also found that periods of struggle always precede times of flow, those moments of being so absorbed in what we are doing that we experience another level of energized focus and enjoyment. Our best moments usually come after times when we find ourselves on the brink of giving up, perhaps because those are the moments when we stop relying on our strength and let God get to work. In 2 Corinthians 12:9, the apostle Paul promises that God's power works best in weakness. Periods of struggle are reminders to let God do the God stuff. That's the antidote to imposter syndrome.

## Making It Practical

DONOVAN

Let's be real. A chapter like this is nothing but a locker-room pep talk without some practical steps to bring it home. Embracing our unique design takes consistent effort, which begins with examining the ideas about ourselves we've picked up along the way. All of us have them, but we didn't choose most of them. These ideas came from parents and teachers, siblings and friends, authority figures such as pastors and even politicians, who all told us something about ourselves that stuck with us. Some ideas were good, but a lot of them were completely off base. Yet they kept hanging around in our minds long enough to get promoted to management in the form of a belief. In business, it's hard to fire a manager, and in life it is just as hard to dislodge a belief. The process starts with bringing in a new set of ideas and reminding ourselves of them over and over until they replace the old management team.

The question is how.

In the old days before we all carried computers around in our pockets in the form of our phones, I encouraged my coaching clients to use Post-it Notes to write out reminders and hang them in all the places they spent the most time. The downside of Post-its is that they eventually become part of the scenery and we stop noticing them. Today, instead of Post-its, I use my phone, setting up three or four alarms a day with messages I write to myself to counteract any area of identity I struggle to embrace. For example, if you struggle with feeling as though you are not good enough, create an 8:00 a.m. notification that says something like this: "My uniqueness is my gift." Set another notification for noon that says, "My struggles today are preparing me for wins tomorrow." I like to use Scripture as a way of basing my beliefs in God's truth, which is why I set my final message, around bedtime, with something like "I am fearfully and wonderfully made." The point is to make the reminders say something meaningful for you. Focus on areas of struggle and doubt and on those things that make you want to give up. This is more than positive thinking. It's a way of rewiring your brain by absorbing truths in the way you most need them at the moment. The more you rehearse the truth about who you are, the less you'll feel the urge to rehearse being somebody else. That truth will unlock your gifts, quiet the urge to measure yourself against everybody else's highlight reel, and even help you see the struggles, setbacks, and sacrifices all as part of the strategy. Day by day you'll lean farther and farther away from performing and start living in the flow of your unique design. And that loud, nagging imposter voice? It won't just fade, it'll get drowned out by the confidence of finally and fully believing you can be who God created you to be.

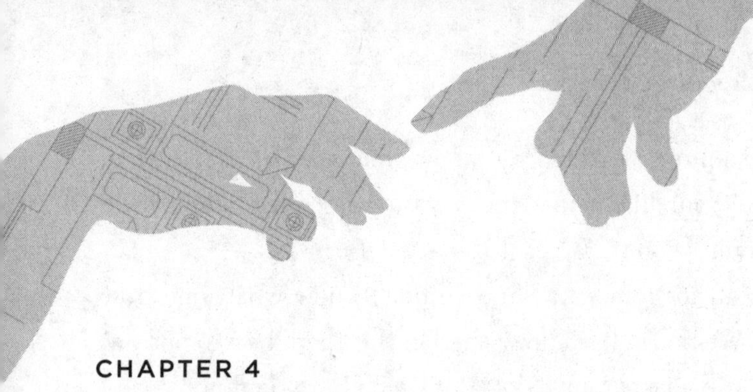

CHAPTER 4

# APPRECIATE WHERE YOU ARE IN YOUR JOURNEY

Our journeys shape us. Every success, every failure, every step forward, every step back changes us. Relationships mold us along with the risks we take and the challenges we shrink from. Where we live now and where we grew up and every place we've been in between leave their marks on us. For better or worse, our journeys—and our origin stories—shape us.

Yet our journeys are not just roads we run down to chase our dreams. Every step of the journey is also a destination. We all have plans and goals, but we have no idea how any of them will turn out. Where you are right now—not where you think you are going—is your only certainty. The Bible puts it this way: "Look here, you who say, 'Today or tomorrow we are going to a certain town and will stay there a year. We will do business there and make a profit.' How do you know what your life will be like tomorrow? Your life is like the morning fog—it's here a little while, then it's gone" (James 4:13–14 NLT).

We plan for tomorrow, but we don't know what tomorrow will hold. We don't even know whether there will be a tomorrow. We're certainly not promised it. But we do have right now—and everything that led up to this moment. None of us were dropped down from a vacuum into the space we occupy. For better or worse, our journeys have led us here. The paths that brought us here shaped us into who we are right now.

A key component of aligning your understanding of who you are with your authentic self is to appreciate and accept where you are and who you are right now, apart from where and who you hope to be in the future. Only then are you ready to succeed.

For the driven among us, thinking in these terms requires a mind shift. Most of us instinctively look ahead. We build on momentum while plotting a course for the future. We are conditioned to live out Newton's first law, which says that a body in motion will stay in motion unless acted upon by an external force, and a body at rest will stay at rest. We have to keep moving, advancing toward our goals. Even when we pause and reflect, we do so to recount the lessons from yesterday that we can use as we chase tomorrow. We can appreciate where we are in our journeys as long as where we are is temporary. If every step of the journey is a destination, we have innumerable destinations left to put behind us.

Whether or not we want to admit it, though, all of us will come to a place where we feel stuck. Forward motion stops and frustration sets in. If you've never been there, you will be, and if you are there now, you can probably point to one of the following three factors that brought your success journey to a halt.

### Factor 1: Your Well-Thought-Out Plans Did Not Go the Way You Were Convinced They Would

DONOVAN

It took me five years to finally quit dancing at the strip clubs. Doing so was a very spiritual decision that came after long periods in the presence of God. But I didn't just walk away. I walked away for a reason. All my adult life I longed to have a wife and family. I knew that my dream was never going to come true as long as I was in the clubs. That was my bargain with God. I'd give up doing something I was very successful at in exchange for the one thing I wanted more than anything else. Twenty years later I'm still single, but my plans fell apart long before the reality that I may never be married set in.

Because my decision to quit dancing was so directly tied to my relationship with God, walking away from the clubs gave me an even greater sense of spiritual zeal. One day while reading my Bible, I came across the passage in Matthew 10 where Jesus sent out his twelve disciples to announce that the kingdom of heaven is near. Jesus told them not to take along any money or even a change of clothes. Instead, he said, "Whenever you enter a city or village, search for a worthy person and stay in his home until you leave town. When you enter the home, give it your blessing. If it turns out to be a worthy home, let your blessing stand" (vv. 11–13 NLT). Those verses jumped off the page at me. I didn't have any obligations holding me in any one place. I didn't have a job and I could not keep my apartment, because I had given away most of my savings. I was broke. I felt like I was in the perfect position to live out the instructions Jesus gave his disciples. I was going to become a vagabond for Jesus. I planned to pack everything I owned into my truck and go from one friend's house to the next as God's vessel to bestow blessings on others. My mom hated the idea, but that didn't stop me. I figured I would sleep on friends' couches when I could, and sleep in my truck when I had to, all to do whatever God wanted me to do and bless whoever I could along the way.

I put my plan into action on a Sunday. I packed my truck and took off for a friend's house. I was about halfway to my friend's house when the temperature gauge on my truck started flashing. Now, keep in mind that this wasn't just any old truck. I drove a flashy bright red customized Ford Expedition with a lift kit, custom wheels, and a certified sound system. It was a sexy beast of a ride that went with my provocative oasis of an apartment that was my personal definition of enticing. The apartment was gone, along with the flat-screen televisions and custom couch, but I still had my truck, which was now giving me trouble for the first time.

The temperature gauge kept climbing, so I took the next exit and pulled into the first parking lot I came to. When I stopped the truck, it went into a full overheating meltdown. I could not believe it. I was just a couple of exits from my friend's house, so I called her and had her come get me, leaving my truck filled with all my earthly possessions sitting in some parking lot near the freeway. First thing the next morning I called a mechanic. But it was a holiday Monday, the last day of a three-day weekend. The mechanic's shop was closed. I kept calling around but I had no luck. By the time I finally went back to the parking lot, my truck had already been towed away. *At least it will be safe in an impound yard*, I thought. When I finally got to my truck, I found I was sadly mistaken. Before the tow truck had hauled it away, someone had already broken into it. Everything I owned in the world was gone. Graffiti covered the bright red paint with metallic flakes that once made my truck almost glow. The custom wheels were gone. There was a hole in the dashboard where my killer sound system had once been. I felt sick to my stomach. Even if I'd had the money to get my truck out of the impound lot, which I didn't, I could never afford to fix all the damage, much less replace my stuff. I had no choice but to walk away empty handed.

Nothing made sense. "I quit the club for you," I yelled at God. "I'm trying to do what is right, but everything is going wrong!" I wish I could tell you that this story had a quick happy ending where God answered my prayers and my life took an immediate turn for the better. Instead, losing my truck was only the first in a long line of episodes where absolutely nothing I had planned worked out the way I'd hoped it would. I was stuck, and I stayed stuck for a couple of years. I had zero prospects for the future, only a present I couldn't escape.

Years later, not long before Kevin and I started writing this book, I started writing another one titled *The Stripped Club: Lost It All Trying to Gain It All, Wondering If It Was All Worth It*. The more I talk to people from different sectors, the more

I understand how common my experience is. We all have big dreams and huge plans only to have life take turns we never expected, leaving us wondering whether it was all worth it. Instead of winning, we lose. Instead of achieving success, we wallow in failure. We expected satisfaction, maybe even happiness, only to experience disappointment and regret, sometimes even when we did win or achieve success. We set our sights on one destination only to find ourselves somewhere we never wanted to go, or we reached our goal only to find it was not what we thought it would be. As a result, we will do almost anything to get out while cursing the journey that led us there.

In my experience, nothing feels more like a betrayal than when life does not turn out like I expected. I blamed God. Some people blame their parents. Or their bosses. Or a teacher or a friend or anyone else who may have had a hand in derailing their dreams.

You may not have lived through this experience yet, but most of us will at some point. It doesn't just happen to those who strike out with the bases loaded or fumble the ball as the clock expires. Even those who hit the winning shot feel like anything but a success when what they expected would happen afterward didn't live up to the hype they built up in their minds. Losers aren't the only ones who question where their journey has brought them. Winners do as well. For many of us, that's the experience that leads us to pick up a book like this one. We want a way out, a way forward, into something real. But getting out is not always, or maybe ever, what we need. Appreciating where the journey has brought you means accepting the loss of your plans and opening yourself up to other possibilities.

### Factor 2: You Are Stuck in a Place That Is Well Below Your Abilities and Potential

DONOVAN

Proverbs 19:21 says, "Many are the plans in a person's heart, but it is the Lord's purpose that prevails." That verse hit me differently when I contemplated what followed my decision to become a vagabond for Jesus. If I had not lost my truck, I never would have ended up sleeping on my sister's couch. I also would not have ended up walking everywhere I went except for those rare days when I could scrape together enough money for bus fare. Nor would I have ended up moving from my sister's couch to my grandmother's couch when I went to work for my grandfather. And I mean work. I didn't have a job description beyond doing whatever my grandfather needed me to do that day. Every day was different.

My grandfather was an interesting man. He left home at the age of fourteen. He started off picking cotton and eventually found his way to California, where he picked oranges. Later he worked on road crews before scraping together enough money to start his own construction business. Eventually he started a church, where he served as pastor while also still doing construction along with owning several rental properties.

When I showed up for work, I never knew whether I was going to be up on a roof laying shingles or fixing something in the church or working on someone's car or sorting through pallets of nearly expired food from Ralphs or Safeway that my grandfather's church then sold in the neighborhood at super-discounted prices. Whatever I had to do that day, we started early in the morning, never stopped for any kind of break or lunch, and worked into the evening before getting up the next day to do it again.

Looking back, I realize my grandfather's intent was to mold me into what he believed a man should be: someone who works hard, puts others before himself, and never thinks any job is beneath him. I hope the lessons took, and I appreciated what he was doing, but installing toilets or fixing shingles in the middle of summer or sorting through piles of half-rotten produce wasn't exactly my idea of a dream job. Eventually I got tired of walking a few miles from my grandmother's house to the church. With no other option, I cleaned out an old storage space in the church basement and moved in there. I found a workout bench somewhere and moved it in along with an air mattress with a slow leak. The church didn't have a shower, which meant I had to go to a gym to shower. Thankfully, I still had a membership, because I'd paid for a couple of years in advance when I still had money. What little money I made didn't last long, thanks to the bills I still had to pay. I often scraped change out of the ashtrays in my friends' cars for cheap tacos at Del Taco or I ate leftover hot dog buns with ketchup and mustard in the church kitchen. No hot dogs. Just the buns with ketchup and mustard. I used to joke with my friends that this was my manna from heaven. It shouldn't have sustained me, but it did.

To say I was stuck in a place that was below my abilities and potential is an understatement. Eventually I discovered that God's purpose was better than my plans, but that came later. In the meantime I found myself in the same place maybe you find yourself, stuck in a career that does not fully utilize your abilities or maximize your potential. Maybe your position did not start this way. You may have landed your dream job, one that stretched you to your limits. Over time, however, you grew while your job did not. The situation became unbearably frustrating when you watched others advance past you while you were still stuck. Maybe you find it difficult to appreciate where you are on this journey when where you are does not appreciate you. At best you feel taken for granted, at worst forgotten. The longer you remain stuck in this space, the more you feel the third factor that makes appreciating where you are now nearly impossible.

### Factor 3: You Feel Like a Failure

DONOVAN

You don't have to fail to feel like a failure. In my experience, the two are often unrelated. I have clients who come to me who are, by every measure, successful, but they don't feel it emotionally. Instead, they look in the mirror and see someone who has not measured up to the standards they set for themselves, someone who may have put together a stellar professional career at the cost of their personal lives, scoring a win, but it has come harder for them than for others they compare themselves with.

I also see those who feel like a failure because they fit the definition. They failed and now believe they are a failure. In the two years I spent living in a storage room in the basement of my grandfather's church, that was me. I basically had nothing. I had no prospects for the future. My goal in leaving the clubs had been to find someone I could share the rest of my life with, but that search crashed into a dead end. I was a failure. No one who looked at my life objectively could reach any other conclusion.

Earlier in this chapter, we wrote that appreciating where you are in your journey requires a mind shift. I learned this lesson in that church basement. I discovered that what we think we are doing and what it looks like we are doing and what God says we are doing are three different things. I thought I was working for my grandfather while also trying to exercise the entrepreneurial spirit inside me by starting a personal training business with one of my few possessions, the workout bench. To those on the outside it probably looked as though I was one step above homelessness, living in a church storage room and working odd jobs for an old man who hired me only because I was his grandson. But what God said I was doing had nothing to do with either of those. That realization changed my life.

I had some dark days down in that basement. The clock was ticking and I was getting no closer to the dreams I had set for myself. Instead, I was sinking deeper and deeper into the wilderness I found myself in. I prayed a lot, but my prayers alternated between complaining to God and giving him detailed instructions on how to fix my situation. I was living in survival mode and I was tired of it. But one day God stopped me in the middle of my self-centered prayers. He made me sit and look at where I was. Everything I'd had and everything I had been was now stripped away. (The irony of this ex-stripper being stripped of all I had was not lost on me.) As I surveyed all that felt like loss and failure, I sensed God whisper to me, "Donovan, you will never know what is within you until you have to live without." Those words changed my life.

God had taken away everything so that I could see how

he had really made me. Over the course of several years I had acquired so much stuff that I could not focus on anything else. So God took it all away. During a later career as a professional photographer, I learned that the key to focus is to blur everything else. Since I could not blur out everything else in my life, God did it by taking it all away. What I thought was failure was actually a necessary part of my development. Only after I could sit and accept where I was could I even begin to think about what was next. Why? Because in the moment of being stuck, of losing it all, only then did I understand who I was and my purpose for being. I discovered what was within me only by living without.

This realization transformed the way I looked at both my journey and where I was. My journey inevitably led me to that basement, which reassured me that nothing in my past was wasted. All of my experiences, both good and bad, had purpose and meaning if I allowed them to. I came to understand that we cannot change what happened to us in the past, but we can determine what we make of it. The land we need to conquer, the battle we need to win, is not on the outside. It's within our minds. Our perspectives, not our circumstances, are what need to change. Living in a church basement and sleeping on an air mattress with a slow leak was not a problem to be solved but a situation to be understood. It revealed something about me that I could not learn any other way.

When I understood my present moment in this way, I realized I had been set free from the hurts and resentments and unmet expectations of the past. I was also freed from being entangled in the pride and materialism that can accompany success. My experiences had humbled me. I think my basement experience also finally allowed me to understand the words of the apostle Paul in Philippians 4:11: "I have learned to be content whatever the circumstances."

Good and bad, success and failure—all have meaning and purpose when viewed as what God is doing to shape and refine me. That understanding came from God as an offering to me that now informs all my beliefs and decisions.

## From Theory to Practice

DONOVAN

None of this dawned on me all at once. I didn't experience a burning-bush moment. My understanding unfolded slowly over time. Even after I sensed God telling me that I would never know what is within me until I had to live without, a switch did not flip, nor were all my problems immediately solved. Instead, this understanding gave me a framework with which I could evaluate both my past and my present and give me a perspective that would carry me into the future, whether that future brought good or bad. Out of this grew a series of questions we all need to ask ourselves throughout our journeys, questions that enable us to look beyond our circumstances to the bigger, overarching purpose of our lives.

The first question is simply this: What lessons has your journey taught you thus far? With every destination you reached, ask yourself what you learned. The answer can be as basic as "Don't try that again." Focus on asking what you learned about yourself, about other people, about God, and about life in general. You don't need to overspiritualize or overthink the question. Think basic. What did you learn that you can take with you on the next step of your journey?

The second set of questions goes a little deeper: How has where you are now prepared you for what may lie ahead? What perspectives have changed? Before you reached the place where you are now, you thought one way and believed one set of beliefs. How has the present changed those? What abilities and capabilities have been revealed? You don't know what is within until you live without. If you've gone through a time of loss, what did you find inside you? Times of loss are not the only teaching moments. What have you learned through the wins and successes? What passions and burdens were unearthed in you that you were not aware of before? The answers to these questions will often change the direction of your life because they not only reveal your heart but also give hints of your purpose for living.

The idea of purpose opens up the final question: What overarching purpose for your life do you see unfold as you look back at where you have come from? Too often we think of purpose as something we have to figure out before we can move ahead. But the easiest way to see your purpose for today and tomorrow is to look back at your journey, as well as the place where you now find yourself. What purpose do you see unfolding over time? What places and situations do you consistently find yourself in? Our journeys are not random, nor are they totally within our control. Much of what happens to us is beyond any of the choices we make. As you look over your journey, you will see the hand of God moving you. This dynamic takes place throughout the Bible, for example, in the story of people like Joseph in

Genesis 37–50. The climax of Joseph's story comes in Genesis 50:20, where he tells his brothers, who sold him into slavery, "You intended to harm me, but God intended it for good." Joseph discovers his purpose through the hardships he endures, which, in the end, result in the saving of hundreds of thousands, if not millions, of lives.

The key to accepting and appreciating where you are right now, like the key to Joseph's experience, is the decision to align your mind with your design and then see your circumstances as the place where you can live out God's purpose and plan.

Our journeys shape us, and we decide what shape they will take, either positive or negative. We cannot change what has happened, but we can decide how we will respond to it. Nothing in our journeys is wasted if we allow it to mold us into the individuals we hope to be. Only when we do that are we ready to take the next step and imagine our potential.

CHAPTER 5

# IMAGINE YOUR POTENTIAL

KEVIN

As I previously mentioned, I grew up hearing my mother tell me, "Whatever you do, be extraordinary and uncommon." Rather than some impossible standard, her words were more of an invitation to explore every possibility and take advantage of every opportunity. When I showed musical promise at a very young age, my parents signed me up for piano lessons. They bought me a saxophone and found the best teachers for me, which allowed me to excel. They did the same with the cello, enrolling me in lessons and camps taught by college-level teachers. They also paved the way for me to excel academically by sending me to Phillips Academy, Andover, one of the top boarding high schools in the country, and later to Yale, an Ivy League university. When I told my parents I wanted to spend a semester studying abroad in China, they encouraged me. They didn't just tell me to be extraordinary and uncommon, they made it possible.

As a result, potential and possibilities have always felt limitless to me. I've already written about how I planned to go to medical school and become a doctor. I also enjoyed my East Asian studies classes and had great experiences in Beijing with the US Embassy, which made me think about a career in foreign service and diplomacy. While studying in China, I also discovered Xiangsheng, or crosstalk, a traditional Chinese comedy with two people talking back and forth. Think Abbott and Costello's "Who's on First?" in Chinese. People told me I had a knack for the language, which made me consider going back to China after college and studying Xiangsheng seriously. As a young adult I had so many possibilities in front of me that it was both exciting and overwhelming. How could I possibly figure out what I should do with my life?

No matter what inspirational speakers may say, we cannot have it all. I could not have a medical practice while touring with Pentatonix while also traveling back and forth to China for a stand-up career along with working as a diplomat and performing as a concert pianist and saxophonist and cellist and excelling as a husband and father. Every human being faces the same basic limitations of time and space and energy and focus. To do anything really, really well, we have to choose where to invest our time, our energy, and our lives. But how do we choose? Or does the thing choose us? Or is something even greater at work? Where do we even begin to look when imagining our potential and the impact it might have? For me, the answer unfolded in a place I never expected.

## Listen to Your Holy Discontent

By November 2013, I was exhausted, but that shouldn't have mattered. As a band, Pentatonix was living the dream. Our music had taken off. We'd spent every month of that year performing all over the United States in sold-out concerts. We had redefined what vocal music could be. That fall we took our show overseas with our first tour in Europe. After shows in Italy, Germany, Austria, and France, we were now in Amsterdam, where we were scheduled for two nights at the iconic 1,500-person venue Paradiso. I should have been on top of the world, but internally, I was spinning. Yes, I saw how my beatboxing contributed to the group's rise. Yes, I was excited. But beneath the success a quiet question kept tugging at me: "Why am I really here?" I had spent twenty-five years becoming a cellist, a scholar, a son of immigrants with a deep sense of mission, and suddenly I was plucked out of that trajectory into something I hadn't envisioned. Was keeping the beat for my bandmates all I had to offer? Was that really my sole purpose?

That night Esther, our tour manager at the time, told us that Justin Timberlake was performing his 20/20 Experience World Tour across town at the Ziggo Dome, a seventeen-thousand-person arena, and invited us to go. Of course we said yes. I had no idea that one night would reroute my entire life. I had never been to an arena concert before or witnessed artistry on that scale. From the first beat, I was amazed. The musicianship. The stage design. The musicians' showmanship: They were playing *and* dancing like nothing I had seen before. The way all of the elements of the show fused to create something greater than the sum of its parts. This was more than a show, it was a revelation. Watching the crowd lose itself in the music, watching how JT reimagined his own hits, I felt something ignite, as though something in me had finally been named.

My bandmates and I were on fire when we piled into the car after the concert. The buzz was electric. No one could stop talking about what we had just experienced, except me. I sat still, staring out the window, too caught up in what I had seen to utter a word, until it finally burst out of me: "That's what I want to do with my life!"

Everyone laughed. "You want to do what, exactly, Kevin?"

"Be an artist."

Everyone laughed again. "Hey, Kev, what do you think you've been doing since you joined the band?" one of my bandmates said. "Dude, you *are* an artist."

I laughed along with them and didn't press the issue, but inside I was screaming, *No, you don't get it! I don't want to just perform. I want to create. I want to pour my soul into something and give people a transcendent experience. I want to channel everything God has placed inside me—the classical training, the modern sounds, the cultural collisions, the faith—and somehow turn that into sound.* But how?

That was the real question: How would I even begin? What was my sound? What kind of artist was I? I didn't sing (not really). I was a professional beatboxer who also played the cello. I loved classical music, but also hip-hop beats, and dance, and pop, and even electronic. Should I mash them all together? Should I just make a cello-beatboxing album? Was that even enough? The possibilities felt endless and, honestly, overwhelming.

That's the tricky part about potential. When it first hits you, it doesn't show up as a perfectly wrapped plan. It often arrives as a holy discontent, a whisper from God that says, "There's more." But stepping into that more requires trust, a narrowing that feels not like loss but like alignment. I knew I couldn't find my sound—or even my potential—without God guiding me through the noise. Later, I had to ask, "Lord, what have you put inside me that the world needs to hear? What does heaven sound like through me?"

All of us have different gifts and abilities. But imagining your full potential means more than letting your imagination run wild with all you could possibly do. Instead, it begins with feeling the weight of your own personal "there's more" moment. Have you experienced this holy discontent? If so, when did it arrive? What did your whisper from God tell you? You have the potential to do any number of things and possibly do them well. But that holy discontent moment—that whisper from God—awakens more than talents and possibilities. It is the first step through the door of discovering your purpose, which flows out of your design. It encompasses all your potential and focuses it in a way that brings out the best and the most from you. Yet to truly discover your purpose and maximize your potential, you have to align yourself with the Creator. Alignment occurs when you properly position your mind, body, and spirit to receive what God has in store for you in his service. It simply means "I'm going to trust his way for me." It acknowledges that he is the one who has placed the giftedness and the yearning for more within you, and it trusts him to make it a reality.

Imagining your potential begins with a whisper from God, but the whisper is only that, a whisper. In our experience, the full details are never revealed. That can present a dilemma for those of us who want a well-thought-out schematic before proceeding. We want to make sure that all our steps will lead to our desired goals. We want to get it right. As a result, we often find ourselves stuck in one place, waiting for full instructions, when really what we need to do is move forward as each step is revealed.

## Open Yourself to Possibilities

KEVIN

When I combined beatboxing and the cello, I did something that, to my knowledge, had never been done before. I had seen videos of Akil Dasan, a musician I looked up to, beatbox and play acoustic guitar on YouTube early in my career, which inspired me. But within classical music, cello-boxing was new. Innovative. Potentially divisive. But more than anything, it was me. I combined two of my passions that inhabited different worlds inside me into one artistic expression.

What I felt that night in Amsterdam at the Justin Timberlake concert went to a different level. I felt like I was now standing in front of a block of marble with a chisel in one hand, a hammer in the other, about to go to work to discover what else might be inside me: passions, abilities, art that I'd seen before only in the shadows. Bringing those parts of me to light meant I had to chip away everything else. I knew only one way to do that: experiment, try, risk, fail, and learn, on repeat. When I fused the cello with beatboxing, those five steps felt even riskier, because they required me to surrender control over the process and trust God instead. And yet I knew it was the only way forward. If I truly believed that God had formed me with purpose (Jer. 1:5) and had plans for my good and my future (Jer. 29:11), then I knew I could trust the Holy Spirit to guide my process.

And yes, failure is a vital part of it. Risking failure by trying something new will not threaten your purpose, it will reveal it. Even closed doors or awkward attempts can hold keys to the next stage of your journey to success. Instead of being paralyzed by the vast possibilities, lean in to them.

For me, that meant doing things I had never prioritized before. I started going to concerts—a lot of them! Stromae. Bruno Mars. Maroon 5. Concert halls became my classroom, and I studied each artist as though I were in a master class: Stromae's mystery and movement, Bruno's charisma and command, the way every moment onstage was designed to create connection. Growing up, I was so focused on academics that I didn't give myself permission to absorb live artistry like that. But now I treated it as research, building an arsenal of inspiration that could help shape the kind of performer I wanted to be.

And then I just started creating. No mic. No recording studio. Just GarageBand on my laptop coupled with a whole lot of curiosity. I made track after track, often clumsily. One of those early efforts became "Renegade," a cello-boxing composition I proudly shared with the rest of Pentatonix in 2014. They loved it. But when I tried performing "Renegade" live on our tour, I bombed. The piece was too complex. I kept messing up onstage. I could have been embarrassed and considered the whole experience a failure, but that moment was gold. My failures onstage taught me to simplify the music without sacrificing artistry, to design music that felt virtuosic, but was still playable. That one mistake-laden piece helped define the next. And the next. And the next. Which ultimately led to my first solo album.

That's the thing about opening yourself up to possibilities and experimenting with your potential. There is no such thing as failure, only spiritual R&D. Even when the crowd doesn't get it, even when you fall short, it's not the end, it's data. And data, in the hands of God, becomes direction.

---

**DONOVAN**

Experiment, try, risk, fail, and learn all come together as you expose yourself to possibility. All are nerve wracking because they drag us out of our comfort zones. They demand acting on an idea of what may be possible, because effort reveals more than a theory ever can. It's not enough to imagine possibilities. You have to move in a direction to discover and verify what you can do. And this, I find, is the sticking point for many of us. Why? We have been conditioned to believe that whatever we try, we have to get it right on our first attempt. We want mastery immediately, because nothing feels worse than failure. Yet that fear only keeps us from discovering who we are and the depth of our potential. As Kevin said, failure is data, it's research. If you don't get something right the first time or the fiftieth, it doesn't matter as long as you reflect and learn from each attempt. You have to give yourself permission to explore, to embrace an educated guess about who you are and what you can do. Then act without worrying about what others may think.

Over the course of my adult life, this has been my philosophy. I approach all of life as an explorer of myself. I've been a model; a dancer; an exotic entertainer; a car salesman; a data processor; a janitor; a personal trainer; a professional photographer; a case manager for homeless families; a panelist on various topics such as men's mental health, entrepreneurship, and dating and marriage; and an internationally traveled certified life coach. I also passed the test for a real-estate license, and I have recently become a certified user experience designer (UXD).

From the outside looking in, you might think I had trouble making up my mind about what I wanted to be when I grew up. That's not how I see it. Instead, I've been excavating the terrain of my identity, passions, and interests by opening myself to possibilities by asking, "Can I do this?" Every step of this journey has revealed to me something new about myself.

Modeling taught me the art of embracing my unique design. I fell two inches short of the industry-standard six feet, but I went for it anyway and learned I had something special that captivated people.

Being an exotic dancer taught me the art of influence. Although it took me a while to learn to use that ability for good, I still gained invaluable insight on how to properly maximize my moments in the spotlight to move crowds toward my desired goal.

Being a car salesman at a no-haggle car dealership started me on my journey of developing my active-listening and empathy-mapping skills.

I did not realize in those moments that those different skills were being refined, but that's the beauty of exploration. We often pick up tools and grow in ways that only time can reveal as profitable.

Working as a data processor further grounded me in discipline.

Being a janitor taught me the art of maintaining an environment and shaped my understanding of what is now my coaching philosophy: Nothing can exist without an environment for it to exist in.

Being a personal trainer taught me how to cultivate real connections and relationships with people, a skill I use daily as a life coach.

My training to become a professional photographer taught me focus and enhanced my instincts. This is where I learned to distinguish between what's worth capturing and what's just background noise.

My time as a case manager for homeless families forever grounded my perspective in gratitude and also exposed me to the importance of community. Those years helped develop one of my leadership-coaching curricula, CARE: Creating a Resourceful Environment.

Every job I had, every career path I traveled, molded me in beneficial ways. It wasn't always obvious, but eventually each season brought clarity and exposed weaknesses. Imagining and realizing my potential—what I do and don't like, what boundaries need to be set to protect and preserve my identity and values—came from allowing the divine gravitational pull to move me into areas of interest and seasons of development that logic alone would not have drawn me into. Each one was worth the risk.

### Learn to Leverage Your Limitations

People who avoid obstacles starve their creativity. If you never slam into a wall, you will never know the joy of figuring out how to get around or over or under it or to bust right through it. Obstacles, both those devised by others and those that arise out of your own limitations, are the environment where potential is realized, because they force you to depend on more than yourself.

Facing forces beyond your control pushes you to rely on God, which deepens your faith and sharpens your focus. This partnership births a creativity that leads you to find solutions where only limitations existed before. Obstacles are never dead ends. They are opportunities to showcase what life has taught you. This is more than a pep talk that Kevin and I give ourselves when times get hard. It's a way of life that offers us new and exciting ways to succeed.

KEVIN

Even though I was a professional musician in the most successful a cappella group in history, I continued to feel a holy discontent. Deep down, I wanted to express myself through music not just by beatboxing or playing cello but with my actual voice. While I was slowly realizing that vocals were just one layer in the rich tapestry of creative art, I also came face to face with a much bigger truth: My voice wasn't my only limitation.

I didn't really know how to produce.

I didn't know how to write great songs.

I didn't even know what melodies worked best for *me*.

Basically, I *didn't* know more than I knew, which should have stopped me in my tracks, but it didn't. Instead of running away, I dove into the depths of my limitations.

After Pentatonix finished our debut original album in 2015, I connected with some of the producers and songwriters from our sessions to see whether they would write with me solo. They graciously said yes even though I hadn't earned my solo stripes yet. These were high-level creatives who worked with artists who were already defined. And here I was, unsure about the art I should make. Some of the songs we made? Let's be real, they weren't great. And that stung. And it kept stinging. For the next seven years, from 2015 to 2022, I kept hearing the same message from people I trusted: You're not there yet. Keep searching.

That phrase could have broken me, but it didn't. I didn't allow it to. Every song that missed the mark still taught me something. Every demo that didn't land still helped chisel away part of the marble. I didn't feel as unsettled anymore. Slowly, the shape of *my* sound was emerging. Slowly, I was partnering with God in uncovering who I was as an artist, not trying to impress him or anyone else but working with him as a co-creator.

Finally, during our 2024 Christmas tour, I was walking with

my friend Shileta Cesario, a soul I'd met through my bandmate Matt. I opened up to her about feeling the weight of my vocal limitations, how hard it was to reconcile my voice with the vision I had for my music. She looked at me and said something that stopped me cold: "You know, sometimes people make an altar in their gifts." Shileta didn't have to explain. I knew exactly what she meant. So many people, especially in entertainment, glorify their talent as the source of their identity, the proof of their worth. When the gift flows easily, they can build their whole self around it. But that altar? It leaves no room for God.

That wasn't my story. I knew I needed him. I *still* need him.

That's why the limitations exist: not to shame us but to shape us. To keep us in alignment. To keep us humble. To keep us dependent. This allows us to leverage our limitations.

Allow your strengths and your weaknesses to keep you in alignment with God. Lay both on the altar. Ask God what he wants to build in you with what you have *and* what you lack, "for it is God who works in you to will and to act in order to fulfill his good purpose" (Phil. 2:13). You will discover that when you hand him your limitations, you're not giving him your weaknesses. You're giving him space to show his glory. That's how it was always designed to be.

## Identify Your Heart's Burdens

KEVIN

When I first started writing songs, I thought the goal was to write hits. And technically some of them *sounded* like hits: They had the "right" chords, a decent hook, a decent vibe. But something about them felt hollow. It wasn't that they were bad, it's that they didn't say anything. I'd walk into writing sessions and ask, "So what should we write about?" And just like that, out came a generic pop track.

It felt as though I was saying everything and nothing at all.

My manager at the time heard all of this in every demo I sent him. That's why he kept saying, "You haven't found it yet." After telling me this for a very long time, he said something new that stunned me: "Why don't you take a step back and just write poems and short stories?"

"What?" I asked, confused.

"Just write what you feel. Write stories from your life. Don't overthink it. Start writing and see what comes out."

I had nothing to lose, so I took his advice. I started writing stories and poems and random thoughts. No filter. No pressure. No chords. No melodies. Just words.

To my surprise, that simple practice ended up becoming one of the most important steps in finding my sound. In those unpolished, unstructured, and unedited stories, I noticed patterns. Certain themes kept rising to the surface.

Family.

Immigrant identity.

The tension of growing up Afro-Caribbean in a Western culture.

The quiet struggle of trying to rise above what I was expected to be.

These weren't just stories. They were burdens: emotional, spiritual, gravitational pulls that had been shaping me for years.

Each story revealed a throughline in my life, the aches that I couldn't ignore. I never saw it clearly until then, but God was using my own life to point me toward my purpose.

In 2017 I had a writing session with Matias Mora and Kameron Alexander. They asked what I wanted to write about. Instead of pitching a song idea, I showed them a couple of the stories I had been writing. Kameron looked up and said, "Wait, these could all be lyrics."

"They're what?" I asked.

"These are your lyrics. Now let's figure out the music that fits."

We then sat down and by the end of the day we'd written "Baba Mi," which means "my father" in my dad's native Nigerian tribal language Yoruba. It explored his struggle of trying to guide a son he'd trained for one path who chose his own instead. The complexity. The love. The cultural tension. That song hit different. And when I sent it to my label at the time, RCA, and my then manager, it was the first time they all said, "Now you're onto something. Keep going."

That's when everything clicked. Before, I had tried to write hit songs that anyone and everyone was supposed to like. Instead, I needed to listen to my burden. Reading back over my stories, I realized I had a burden for people like me, the misfits who live between definitions, who feel as if they don't fully belong to any one culture, space, or identity. That was my story. I didn't feel black enough to fit into one community and felt too black to fit into another. I was too academic for some and yet not academic enough for others. I was too classical for hip-hop and too hip-hop for classical. All my life I had been too this and not enough of that. Even in Pentatonix I often felt like an outsider among my chorally trained, musical-theater-loving partners.

And yet there was that ache—that God-designed ache—I had for others who found themselves in the same predicament. All the "too this" and "not enough" that I had experienced was not an obstacle I had to overcome. It was a blueprint. And when I finally understood that, I knew what I was called to do. My potential became clear when I clearly saw my purpose, my calling: It is to tell stories that help misfits feel seen, that help people understand that their identities, the ones they were told disqualified them, might be the superpowers they were given to transform the world.

When you can finally identify the gravitational pull of the burden within you, your imagination about your potential can take flight. Your burden is usually bigger than you. That's how you know it's real. You won't feel capable of carrying it on your own, and that's the point. It's the thing that keeps you up at night, the area of your heart you keep visiting. It usually comes wrapped in your pain, your mess, your redemption story. For me, it included a whole group of people I instinctively wanted to protect.

Your burden is the root of your calling. It's what God designed in you before you were even born. Jeremiah 1:5 says, "Before I formed you in the womb I knew you." Your burden isn't random. It's divine. And when your burden becomes vision, that vision becomes purpose. And that purpose? It's where your potential comes to life.

This is the power your potential has: not in dreaming of far-off possibilities but in the daily gritty work of partnering with that gravitational pull and trusting that as you move forward, God is lighting the path. And when you start to live out your purpose, you'll gain the greatest, most life-giving form of success you will ever experience.

CHAPTER 6

# PLACE YOURSELF ON A TRAJECTORY FOR SUSTAINED SUCCESS

Back in 1971, amid the media feeding frenzy leading up to Super Bowl V, Dallas Cowboys running back Duane Thomas was asked if the Super Bowl is the ultimate game. He replied, "Well, they're playing it next year, aren't they?"[3] More than fifty years later, they're still playing it again next year.

Neither of us was alive back then, but Duane Thomas summed up the paradox of success better than we ever could. The ultimate goal, whatever it may be for you, is never ultimately the ultimate. For me, Kevin, the Grammy is the ultimate award for a musician. As part of Pentatonix I've won three and was nominated for two more. But as with the Super Bowl, they're giving out more Grammys next year. And aside from the winners, hardly anyone remembers who won last year, or the year before, or the year before that. That's true of every ultimate prize. Don't believe this is true? Answer this question: Without googling, who won Super Bowl V?

This is what makes the quest for success so frustrating. You conquer a peak, achieve your ultimate goal, then turn around and have to start all over again climbing the next one, all the while knowing that most people care far more about what you do next than what you have already done. The stress of extreme peaks and valleys, and even worse, the feeling of being stuck on a plateau, can leave you questioning why you even try.

As we mentioned earlier, our goal in writing this book is to move beyond success peaks and valleys. We don't view success as an end point. We view success as a trajectory, where what matters is whether someone is living closer to their purpose and using more of their potential today than they were yesterday. This is a completely different understanding of success from one defined by chasing goals. For goal setters and overachievers, success usually means pushing yourself to your limits, then pushing some more. But moving to the next level and the next to reach greatness means grinding yourself into the ground, paying any price to move above and beyond your peers. In our experience this idea of success abandons your authentic self to pursue productivity.

A trajectory of sustained success requires hustle and soul. It does not focus on how much you can do. Rather, it focuses on alignment with yourself, with your values, and with your Creator as you live out your purpose every day. Performance itself is not a bad thing if you're performing within this alignment. But our experience has taught us that in the real world these essentials can easily take a back seat to pursuits. Setting goals and aiming high can be healthy, but only if reaching your goals does not cost you your sanity, your identity, or your soul. Staying aligned demands that you remain clear about why you are on this trajectory to begin with.

### 1. Clarify Your Why

DONOVAN

Your why is your deepest reason at the moment for doing what you do. Not just the reason but the deepest reason, the reason upon which every other reason is grounded. More often than not, most of us run around pursuing one thing or another without ever understanding what is really driving us. We mistake the goal for our why without digging deeper inside ourselves to understand why this goal and why pursue it now. Uncovering the deepest reason requires asking ourselves a series of questions that I refer to as the "So that what?" exercise, starting with the most obvious question: "What do I want?"

I am not looking for deep answers such as world peace or clean drinking water for everyone. "What do I want?" means "What do I really want right here, right now? What motivated me to climb out of bed this morning and start this task or do this job?" This is the place for honesty, not philosophy. Begin with what you want, then keep digging by asking, "So that what?"

For example, you may be contemplating a new career path:

***What do you want?***

**A new job.**

***So that what?***

**So that I can make more money.**

***So that what?***

**So that I can buy a new car.**

***So that what?***

**So that I can be taken seriously in my neighborhood.**

***So that what?***

**So that I can be seen as a real man.**

***So that what?***

**So that I can prove my dad wrong.**

Or you want to get healthier:

***What do you want?***

**To start going to the gym.**

***So that what?***

**So that I can get in shape.**

***So that what?***

**So that I can feel healthier in my own skin and get off this medication.**

*So that what?*

**So that I have more energy to show up fully each day for myself and my loved ones.**

*So that what?*

**So that I stop missing a chance to make and be a part of memorable moments because of fatigue.**

*So that what?*

**So that my life becomes less about ensuring I don't get really sick and more about experiencing how good life can be as a healthy person.**

In that first example, we've dug down to the deepest reason for this hypothetical person. The career, the job, the money, the car, the reputation all come back to a broken relationship that cries out to be fixed. All the other answers are secondary. What do you want? The real answer is, "I want to have a real, loving relationship with my father and gain his respect."

Your journey to your why doesn't have to go to such a painful place, but it does need to be this honest. The goal is to dig down to what touches, moves, and inspires you to do what you do and to chase the goals you chase—your deepest reason mentally, spiritually, and emotionally. These connections turn your deepest reason into your true north that transcends everything else in this moment. I say "in this moment" because what touches, moves, and inspires you in your twenties may not be what touches, moves, and inspires you in your thirties or forties or fifties. Life never stands still, and neither do we. As we wrote in chapter 4, every step of our journeys changes us. As we grow and learn and hurt and laugh and experience whatever life brings, our deepest reason grows and develops with us.

Wherever you may be at this stage in life, the point is to clarify your why so that you understand what gives your life meaning and purpose. Understanding your why is useful only if you keep it front and center, which can be tricky while balancing the rest of life's demands. But once you understand your why, you will find yourself moving away from goal chasing to living out your purpose every day. Goals then become what they're meant to be: signposts along the way, not destinations.

## 2. Prioritize Your Essentials and Balance Your Pursuits

KEVIN

I thought I knew what I was getting myself into when our first daughter, Kaia, was born. I can hear all of you veteran parents out there laughing, and that's okay, because I now laugh at how naive I was before we brought Kaia home from the hospital. It's like the old saying goes, every fighter has a plan until they get punched in the nose. That's what a newborn can do to you. Between trying to figure out how to be a dad on the fly, finding time to catch some shut-eye, bonding with my daughter, continuing to build my relationship with my wife, crafting my own sound, all while also trying to keep up with life as a part of Pentatonix, I never knew whether I was coming or going. It felt as though I was living in constant crisis mode. On top of that, my fatigue brought out my familiar inner critic, who constantly told me I should be able to handle everything and that I should be doing more and that I was letting my child down and I was letting my wife down and I was letting my band down, and ultimately I was letting myself down. My life coach told me to give myself grace. But that was hard to do in my frustration over being busier and more flustered than I had ever been in my life while getting so little accomplished.

When my daughter was around nine months old, my wife and I decided we might actually be able to survive going on a much needed vacation to Hawaii with an infant. I had also just finished our band's Christmas tour, our first since COVID, which meant my wife had to be a solo parent for most of November and December. She needed a vacation more than I did, and I didn't know how much longer either of us could survive without one. From the moment we stepped off the plane, I felt myself relax. Throughout our time on the islands, however, we kept crossing paths with one particular man. We saw him so often in so many places that I wondered whether he was following us. I finally stopped the man and struck up a conversation. When he told me he was a pastor from Southern California who was on vacation like we were, I had to laugh. He and I hit it off, and before long I said something about being a new dad and trying to juggle my personal life and career. He looked me in the eye and said something I will never forget: "Kevin, if you don't keep your time sacred, no one else will."

His words hit me like a giant wave crashing onto a beach.

When I got back home to California, I took a long look at my schedule. I started asking myself, "When am I most tired? When do I need to be with my family, not just physically but emotionally? When does my soul most feel the need for rest or fire?" The further I dug into myself, the more I realized I was still trying to conduct my professional life the same way I had when I joined Pentatonix. At the very beginning we all lived in the same apartment complex, ostensibly to save money, but it was more than that. We lived our band life 24/7. We were all young and single and completely focused on making it as a band. All of us poured our entire lives into our music. Fast-forward a decade. Pentatonix had succeeded beyond our wildest dreams, but we still kept in contact as if we were living together. Everyone constantly texted everyone else at every time of day and night about anything and everything—an upcoming tour date or a studio session or a song idea or anything else remotely connected to Pentatonix. As a result, the line between my personal and professional lives hadn't just blurred, it didn't exist! I knew I had to make a change, a big one, to honor this new stage of life I was in.

After much prayer I sent an email to my bandmates. I had no idea how they would take what I had to say, but putting my feelings into words felt liberating. I wrote:

Dear PTX,

I want to start by saying how much I care about each of you. It's an incredible gift to be on this journey together—building something meaningful, pushing each other to grow, and showing up every day with heart and purpose. I'm deeply grateful for what we've built and who we are to one another.

At the same time, I want to share something personal that's been on my heart. Becoming a parent has been the most transformative experience of my life. My children are my greatest joy, but they also challenge me in ways I never imagined—to be more present, more patient, and more intentional. It's become clear to me that in order to be the parent I want to be, and the partner you all deserve, I need to make some changes to how I manage my time and energy.

Starting now, I'm going to be shifting my schedule a bit to create more protected space for my family. After 5:30 p.m., I'll be stepping away from work-related communication to be fully present at home. And in the mornings, I'm going to give myself until around 11:00 a.m. before diving into email and work messages. I've realized I need that time to pour into my home life and refill my own cup so that when I show up here, I'm not running on fumes. You all deserve my overflow, not my exhaustion.

This isn't about pulling away from the work or the mission. If anything, it's about showing up even more rooted, more focused, and more grounded. I believe this shift will make me better in every area of life—including here, with you.

Thank you for your trust, your support, and your grace as I make this adjustment. I'm always here during the core of the day, fully committed, and even more aligned with what truly matters.

With gratitude and love,
KO

To my surprise, everyone, even my managers, responded with grace and understanding. I had also, unknowingly, set a precedent for other members to sit with themselves, dive deep on what they needed to be their best in the band, and ask for it, whether it was time off for parenting or to pursue a solo project or just downtime to recalibrate and reset. Before, no one asked because we all felt guilty, as though we were letting the band down, because our entire lives had been so centered around Pentatonix.

A few days after writing that letter to the band, during an *Imagine Faith Talk* podcast meeting, I told Donovan and Kor, our producer, what I had done. Donovan looked at me, smiled, and said, "That's just prioritizing your essentials and balancing your pursuits."

He then broke it down for me. Donovan explained how essentials are the things that keep me aligned with who I am: God. Worship. My family. My health. Pursuits are the things I feel called to do: music, creative expression, the artistic journey that makes me come alive.

Following a trajectory of sustained success means that when my essentials are in place, my pursuits will flow with purpose.

And when I did clock in with the band, or onstage, or in a studio, I wouldn't be scraping the bottom of the barrel. I'd be offering my overflow. That single word, *overflow,* became my guidepost. It wasn't about doing less. It was about being rooted. It was about showing up with intention, knowing what filled me and what drained me, and crafting my life around what mattered most. I had always believed that work, the grind, the tour schedule, the performance was the goal. But now I see it differently. My essentials are now in this order:

1. God
2. Health in body and spirit
3. Family
4. Creative passion
5. Everything else that comes out of the overflow

My wife Leigh's support through this has meant everything. She knows me well enough to understand that I'm at my best when my time is anchored in what fills me. Her belief in that rhythm gave me the confidence to shape a schedule that honors both my roles as a husband and father and my calling as an artist. I'm not perfect at it. Some days are messy. Some days I overcommit. But I'm learning. And with each day, I try to remember what that pastor said on the shores of Hawaii: If you don't keep your time sacred, nobody else will.

Now I do.

We can't tell you what your essentials should be. That's a decision you must make. I also know that a musical-entrepreneurial career in which I get to set my own schedule is different from most other careers. Most people can't write to their boss and say, "I'm going to work on me till 11:00 a.m." Carving out that space may mean you have to wake up earlier or find another time in the day to prioritize the essentials that give you life. But we can confidently say that when pursuits displace essentials, not only does life get out of balance but also we become less productive no matter how busy we might be. Pursuits need essentials to anchor and drive them.

Pursuits are what we do. Essentials are the why beneath it all. Prioritizing essentials while balancing pursuits allows us to step into a trajectory of success that brings a sustainable inner satisfaction that chasing goals cannot. Remember, pursuits need essentials. Essentials don't need pursuits.

## 3. Take Steps That Will Keep You on a Consistent Trajectory of Success

All of this is great in theory. But in the heat of hitting deadlines and reaching goals while trying to pull the most out of yourself and keeping up with life's day-to-day demands, these ideals can get hazy. We've found three practical steps that quiet the noise and help keep us on a consistent trajectory of success.

### 1. Anchor Yourself in Integrity

The dictionary defines *integrity* as a firm adherence to principles, as well as a sense of wholeness or completeness. The set of higher values from which we operate is the anchor that keeps us from going adrift from our authentic selves. Without it, momentum becomes manipulation, and the end always justifies the means. A trajectory of sustained success refuses to go that route. In our experience we have found that you can move fast and still be honest and true to yourself. Integrity is what ensures that your results are repeatable, because they are built on truth, not tactics.

The enemy of integrity is not compromise as much as it is opportunism. Struggles can tempt us to jettison our values, but nothing puts integrity to the test like opportunity. It is an inherent human weakness going back to the book of Genesis. Satan's first temptation to the first man and woman came as a once in a lifetime offer: Eat this and "you will be like God" (Gen. 3:5). The offer was too good to refuse, and the human race has suffered the consequences ever since. Like Adam and Eve in the garden of Eden, opportunism always feeds on what you feel is the best thing for you right now while offering what looks like a shortcut to your long-term goals. This does not mean we should ignore every opportunity that comes our way. Far from it. But with every door that opens we need to check to see whether going through it keeps us in alignment with who we say we are. Our integrity keeps us focused on the grand scheme of our lives and legacies, which for the Christ follower is to glorify God. Anything that pulls us from that path is not an opportunity but a temptation to lose ourselves in our quest for success.

### 2. Follow the Compass of Your Identity

Our first four chapters focused on discovering your authentic self for a reason. Your identity, the unchanging essence of who

God designed you to be, is your compass. Instead of following trends or spinning around responding to conflicting external demands, this compass cuts through the distractions and points you in the direction of truth. The needle of the compass is your internal resonance—that sense of peace that comes from living in alignment with your God-given values, passions, and purpose. Discerning the direction your compass is pointing requires you to carve out time to filter every decision through a simple set of questions:

- Does this align with who I am?
- Will this lead me toward my purpose or away from it?
- Am I doing this to be seen or because I see clearly?

A sustained trajectory of success allows your identity to move you. It doesn't map out every detail, but it gives you the internal GPS to navigate with peace and precision any terrain over which your journey may take you. Following it will lead to fulfillment, not just achievement.

### 3. Establish and Enforce Clear Boundaries

Boundaries are the parameters that keep our pursuits from outgrowing their importance. Your design for success won't remain aligned without them. Boundaries are not walls as much as they are doors with locks. Instead of locking people out, they keep your peace within, which then allows you to engage with others from the overflow of your life rather than at the cost of what you value most. If you're constantly accessible, you're constantly exhausted. High performance requires energy, and energy requires protection.

For me, Kevin, boundaries are basically a clarity statement I have for myself when it comes to my job. No matter how glamorous life in a successful band may appear from the outside, it is a job. And like every job, there are parts of it I do not love. But here's a liberating truth that boundaries bring: I don't have to love every part of my job to honor it and its purpose in my life. Nor do I have to be in the middle of every creative decision the band makes. When my input is needed, I give it. In areas where I am most passionate, I express it. If anything takes away from my time, my family, my values, or other important parts of my legacy, I'll fight to right it. But in the other areas, I trust my bandmates to make the decisions that will be the best for all of us. Working this way has made me more productive while also guarding me from feelings of resentment or burnout that can plague anyone in any arena.

When you combine these three steps—anchor yourself in integrity, follow the compass of your identity, and establish and enforce clear boundaries—you move into a sustainable level of success. You don't just move fast. You move well. You don't just get results. You get rewarded without regrets. And you won't have to compromise as you climb. There's no roller coaster. Just a sustained success.

CHAPTER 7

# OPTIMIZE YOUR PERFORMANCE

KEVIN

In the middle of a production session in my home studio, my phone buzzed with a FaceTime call from my bandmate Scott. I picked up. "Hey, what's up?" I said.

"I'm sitting here with Lindsey and Craig, and we've been talking about our upcoming Hollywood Bowl show," Scott started, which immediately grabbed my attention. Built in 1922, the historic Hollywood Bowl is *the* concert venue in Southern California and one of the top ten in the entire country. The most iconic artists of all time have performed there. To have Pentatonix join that group was an absolute dream scenario for all of us. Because this was a stand-alone show, we decided that making money wasn't the goal. We would invest the same amount of money we were going to make from the show to create a once in a lifetime experience for our fans, a show unlike anything we had ever done before, and film it. It didn't matter to us that we would break even or lose a bit of money for this opportunity. Our creative directors, Lindsey and Craig, were in the middle of all our planning.

"Okay," I said, waiting for what would come next. Scott never thinks small. He is always, *always* trying to find ways to creatively elevate everything we do as a band to heights no one has ever thought of before.

"And we've been talking about your cello section," Scott said, smiling. Pentatonix shows include a section when I come out onstage alone with my cello and do my patented celloboxing. My solo gives the rest of the band a chance to rest their voices while also showcasing the skills that prompted my bandmates to invite me to join Pentatonix in the first place.

"So, Kevin, we're thinking you should take your segment to a whole new level that's going to blow people's minds."

Now I was excited. "What do you have in mind?" I asked.

Scott grinned. "Why don't you do something with an army of cellos and"—he sort of paused—"a dancer."

I looked at Scott in disbelief. He had no way of knowing I was already experimenting with my own interpretation of Beethoven's Fifth Symphony, which we aptly named "Kevin's Fifth." Johnny May, a friend and music savant I'd invited to work with me on the project, and I were in the middle of working on a demo of that very track when Scott called. Talk about God's divine timing!

"Whoa, Scott, I actually think I may have something perfect for that. Let me send you the track. Call me back after you've had a chance to listen to it."

Five minutes later Scott and the creative directors called again. "Oh. My. Gosh, Kevin. This is *sick*!" he said. "It's perfect. Exactly what we need. Let's get to work on it."

I was just as excited as Scott. He and I, with our creative directors, talked a little longer about both my segment and the entire show. But after our conversation ended, reality hit. I had just agreed to take a fun little piece I was experimenting with in my home studio and turn it into a signature moment in front of thousands of people at the Hollywood Bowl, plus however many hundreds of thousands or millions of people streamed the performance online. *What have I just gotten myself into!* Immediately all my old insecurities came washing over me. *I don't have the skills to pull this off. I am not the kid who practiced enough to do this. I'm not qualified. I'm not this. I'm not that.* I almost had to scream at my mind to be quiet. And then I reminded myself of Kobe Bryant and his Black Mamba mentality that basically said, "Can I do this? I don't know, but I'm going to find out."

I'm no Black Mamba, but right then I decided to align my thoughts about this upcoming performance with my identity in Christ, the values that guide me, and my purpose for being an artist and a human being. The word for this alignment is *optimization*: the process of ensuring I was making the best use of my time, resources, and gifts to become the fullest version of who God was calling me to be for that moment.

Optimization isn't about achieving more. It's about making the most effective use of every situation or resource—both expected and unexpected. More than the ability to rise to a single challenge, optimization is a mindset that is ready for the next challenge and the next, even on those days when the biggest challenge is simply staying engaged in a normal routine. Optimizing your performance requires focusing on self-development: understanding your identity, values, and purpose, then acting on them. It is the next step to living out a trajectory of success that not only brings constant satisfaction but also pulls the best out of you. Donovan and I have identified five principles that will guide you to optimizing your performance.

## Principle 1: Replace Busywork with Breakthrough Work

Dwayne "the Rock" Johnson famously broke down his secret to success to these three things: "Be humble. Be hungry. And always be the hardest worker in the room." Who are we to argue with the Rock? But optimizing your life means far more than simply working harder. Most of us know from experience that you can be insanely busy and still be unfulfilled. Often our schedules are dominated by "urgent" tasks that do not move us any closer to our long- or short-term aims. The process of optimization begins with learning to clearly distinguish busywork from breakthrough work that can truly move the needle. The latter is usually the hardest, but it yields the greatest feelings of flow, peace, and fulfillment.

How do we tell the difference between busywork and breakthrough work? Many of us often get caught up in busywork, tasks that are easier and more distracting, instead of focusing on our breakthrough work that connects us to our deepest goals. Breakthrough work requires focus, energy, and sometimes the willingness to face doubts and fears. Focus is essential because it reveals what matters to us. By asking questions like "What do I want?" and "Why am I doing this?" we gain clarity about our purpose, clarity that fuels our energy and motivates us to pursue breakthrough work. With this understanding, we can better manage our time and energy, ensuring they are directed toward what counts. Ultimately, success comes from having a clear purpose, staying in the flow, and managing our energy effectively. This is how we stay committed to what matters.

Shortly after Scott asked me to create something epic for the Hollywood Bowl, I called Brian, my high-performance coach, to share the news. I was excited and overwhelmed and celebrating and dreading it all at the same time. Brian laughed with me, then asked me a personal question: "You've learned so much personally and artistically over the past few years, but what do *you* want out of this performance? How do you want to feel going through the experience of getting there?" His question stopped me in my tracks. Again. (Brian has a way of doing that.) I'd been so caught up in the magnitude of what lay before me that I was pretty much in survival mode. Up until then all I could think about was trying to get through the performance without embarrassing myself. Now I shifted from survival to intention. I had to define what *my* perfect scenario looked like, one not shaped by comparison or fear or pressure but anchored in who I really am. Before, I had reacted. Now I needed to start acting out of alignment. I began with reflecting on what was motivating me. What was my why?

More than anything, I wanted the entire process to feel like worship, not just for the five and a half minutes I would be onstage but in every rehearsal, every prep session, every moment of doubt and faith. I wanted it all to be an offering to God. For me, being aligned means fulfilling God's purpose in God's timing in the place of his choosing as an offering to him. Seeing the Hollywood Bowl as an opportunity not just to perform but to worship was, for me, the pivot from busy to breakthrough. When I pictured that scenario, I felt like I was flying, because I wasn't anchored in doubt or fear. I was soaring in faith, the faith that gave me energy to go after it.

With my why now clearly defined and elevated to my priority for both my preparation and my performance, I was excited to chart the next steps. Rather than break down my schedule in minute detail, I focused instead on the big moves I needed to make. What were three or four actions I must do to get where I needed to go? As I looked ahead to the Hollywood Bowl performance, these were my steps:

1. Brainstorm the track and concept.
2. Produce the track.
3. Practice the track.
4. Simulate the performance.

If these look basic and simple, there's a reason for that: They are. Simplicity yields clarity, and clarity leads to consistency. Once I had my steps in place, I asked, "Are these connected to who I say I am and who I want to become? Are they aligned with my identity?" The answer to that question lay less in the steps and more in how I carried them out. The temptation to let our egos hijack our performances never leaves. If we give in, we slip into the realm of busywork, pursuing accomplishments that may seem big and important but whose impact is fleeting. Breakthrough work not only pulls the best out of us for short-term goals and projects but also moves us closer to our overarching life goals and purpose. Rather than fleeting, breakthrough work is sustaining and life-giving.

### Principle 2: Use Your Time Intentionally

Ephesians 5:15–17 says, "Look carefully then how you walk, not as unwise but as wise, making the best use of the time, because the days are evil. Therefore do not be foolish, but understand what the will of the Lord is" (ESV). These verses emphasize a purposeful use of the limited amount of time we have each day. "Make the best use of the time" and "understand what the will of the Lord is" go hand in hand. The best use of your time is pursuing God's plan for you. But living out God's purposes for your life doesn't happen by accident. As the old saying goes, if you don't tell your feet where to go, you'll wonder where you are. And if you don't take control of your time, you'll wonder why you can't get anything done.

Intentionality bridges the gap between good intentions and measurable results. When combined with personal alignment, intentionality produces flow, and flow builds momentum that pushes us ever closer to our goals. Practically speaking, making the best use of the time is about more than the old cliché: Failing to plan is planning to fail. Everyone knows the value of setting schedules and creating timetables. Creating plans is easy; carrying them out requires discipline to focus on the most important task at hand instead of trying to accomplish everything that needs to be done everywhere all at once. Many of us take pride in our ability to multitask, yet too often what we think of as multitasking turns into randomly switching from one demand to another without a well-thought-out plan. Nothing kills momentum like randomness. Productivity and flow happen when we bring all our attention to one or two manageable things at a time.

Of course, none of this happens on its own. Intentionality calls for creating road maps, daily, weekly, and monthly, to keep us on track in the flow. When I began preparing for my Hollywood Bowl performance, I took my four primary actions and broke them down into smaller pieces:

**Month 1: Brainstorm Track and Concept**

- Meet with creative directors to discuss orchestra and dancer ideas.
- Build rough track with those visuals in mind.
- Refine both the musical arc and performance flow with team input.

**Month 2: Produce Track**

- Work with Johnny May to produce final version.
- Send to orchestrator for string arrangements.
- Record strings and finalize for musical director.

**Month 3: Practice Track**

- Practice daily cello and beatboxing drills.

- Collaborate with choreographers and dancer.
- Start filming practice sessions, reviewing them, and refining.

### Last Two Weeks: Simulate Performance

- Perform for three or four trusted friends over Zoom and get feedback.
- Rehearse again with corrections and tweaks.

I then created weekly and daily maps to keep myself in the flow. For the week before the performance, my map looked like this:

### Daily Time Block (Sample)

4:15–4:45 a.m. | Worship
4:45–5:00 a.m. | Stretch, mindset video
5:00–7:00 a.m. | Cello practice
7:00–9:00 a.m. | Family breakfast, play, and worship; take kids to school
9:00–11:00 a.m. | Perform for Zoom audience or rehearse PTX music
11:00–11:30 a.m. | Shower, protein shake
11:30–12:00 p.m. | Practice band music in the car while driving
12:00–4:00 p.m. | Full band rehearsal
4:00–5:00 p.m. | Prep road map for next day, dinner, drive
5:00–6:30 p.m. | Workout
6:45–8:15 p.m. | Family time, bedtime routine
8:30 p.m. | Sleep

Now, let me be clear, this schedule reflects my personality and my energetic flow. There's a reason the rest of the members of Pentatonix call me the dad of the group. Whatever your road maps might look like, arrange them in a way that gives your best energy to those projects that make you come alive instead of letting other people's emergencies define your purpose.

Plotting your time takes intentionality. It allows you to make the most of your time by telling your time how you will spend it rather than reacting to whatever crises come your way. It sets you free from stress by making large goals and projects feel less overwhelming. Intentionality also declutters the mind, allowing you to clearly see the goal in a tangible, manageable way. As you move toward the goal, you will feel how this goal is shaping you. Of course the unexpected will come along. As the old saying goes, we plan and God laughs. But when you create a road map focused on both the goal and God's path for you, the unpredictable will not throw you off course.

### Principle 3: Manage Your Self-Talk

In the thick of preparing for the Hollywood Bowl performance—when the deadlines were real and the stakes felt higher than ever—I found myself confronting things I'd never done before. Not just creatively. Internally. I was juggling choreography, original music, complex production, and storytelling in front of tens of thousands of people. And as much as I tried to stay in flow with time blocking, reflection, and execution, there were moments when I felt overwhelmed and a familiar question rolled around in my head: "Am I really built for this?" No matter how hard I tried to ignore it, the doubt just would not go away.

Ignoring doubt won't silence it, but one of the most underrated but powerful practices in your toolkit will: positive self-talk. Proverbs 18:21 says that the tongue has the power of life and death, and this is especially true when we turn it toward ourselves. You cannot optimize your performance if your inner dialogue is working against you. For most of us, that negative inner dialogue will show up at some point as the spokesperson for doubt and fear. Thankfully, we have the power to override doubt and fear by speaking life into ourselves.

Improving your self-talk does not mean hyping yourself up with empty affirmations. All the "You got this!" and "You can do this!" declarations in the world are not enough to allow you to get this or do this. Rather, the kinds of self-talk that override doubt and fear are soul-level reminders of God's purpose and plan for your life. When fear and doubt rise up, we simply remind ourselves of who we were created to be and why we are where we are.

When I started to get overwhelmed by the scope of performing in such an iconic venue in front of so many people, I reminded myself that God had built me for this moment. He trusted me, just like he trusted Adam to name the animals. When I felt like I was in no way up to the challenge, I remembered the Scripture that says that God's strength is made perfect in our weakness (2 Cor. 12:9). God never meant for me to do anything on my own but instead to operate in the strength that he pours out through the Holy Spirit. When the voice of doubt told me I had no business being on the stage of the Hollywood Bowl, I listened instead to Proverbs 3:5–6, which says, "Trust in the Lord with all your heart and lean not on your own understanding; in all your ways submit to him, and he will make your paths straight." God's path had led me straight to this stage; I did not seek it out myself. Since God brought me here, I knew this was my dominion where I was meant to rule.

Effective self-talk is simple, specific, and personal. It's built on God's truth and promises, not on our hopes and desires. When we step into God's truth, we are stepping into the identity God has always spoken over us. For Donovan and me, speaking these powerful truths allows us to feel God's presence—his truth—envelop us. We don't feel the need to prove something. God's truth allows us to go out into whatever arena he has prepared and enjoy the moment. Fear and doubt breed bondage to lies, but truth sets us free to soar.

## Principle 4: Build a Daily Reflection Process

KEVIN

Life moves pretty fast, and the more demanding your schedule, the faster it goes. Time never moved faster for me than it did between the initial FaceTime call with Scott and my performance at the Hollywood Bowl. It wasn't just that my prep time seemed to fly by. Every second of every day I felt like I was jumping from one demand to the next. One moment I was in worship. The next, I was practicing cello with full intensity. Then suddenly I was in family mode. Then rehearsal. Then band meetings. Then prayer again. Then silence. Then noise.

Every moment asked something different of me and carried different energy. I quickly realized that if I didn't honor the transitions between each part of my day, I would end up dragging the unresolved emotions, expectations, or energy from one space into another. Over the course of a day, that disconnection would add up and carry over to the next day and the next and the next until all my carefully made plans turned into chaos. So I had to learn to pause and reflect not at the end of the day but in the transitions throughout the course of the day. I'd stop, place my hand over my heart, and breathe in deeply. As I exhaled, I'd pray, "God, thank you for the period I just had doing X. Now that's done. That chapter is closed." Before stepping into the next, I'd ask myself:

- How do I want to feel going into this next space?
- What does clarity look like in this block?
- What does excellence feel like here?

I then imagined the next block: Me, in the next hour. Not distracted. Not rushing. Not carrying the pressure of the last thing into this one. But fully present. Meticulous. Grateful. Doing the will of the Father in this moment, not the last one.

More than a mental hack, these transitions are sacred moments. As Sister Joan Chittister writes in *The Monastic Heart*, it's a "holy pause." Psalm 46:10 says, "Be still, and know that I am God; I will be exalted among the nations, I will be exalted in the earth." This verse is the very definition of worship. By stopping, closing out one moment and offering the next as an act of worship in the presence of God, I was giving myself a chance to return to clarity—again. To remember who I was—again. And to refocus on my why—again.

Did I always stay undistracted, unrushed, fully free of the pressure of the previous thing, fully present and meticulous and grateful, doing the will of the Father in this moment, not the previous one? Of course not! I'm human after all. But rather than get down on myself and fall back into the trap of negative self-talk, I went through a reflection process developed by Donovan: verify, purify, occupy.

---

**DONOVAN**

One of the most powerful tools I walk clients through when they feel disconnected, disoriented, or unsure of how to move forward is a three-step process I call verify, purify, occupy. It's a grounding framework designed to align you with the optimized version of yourself, the version God intended when he dreamed you into existence. The truth is this: You can't walk in divine alignment if you haven't first checked your inner assignment.

The first step is to verify. This is where you slow down long enough to examine the motives behind your pursuits. Too often, we chase goals based on cultural pressure, unresolved insecurity, or borrowed expectations. Verifying your motives is like double-checking the destination on your GPS before starting the journey. If the address is wrong, speed won't help. Ask yourself, "What do I really want and why do I want it?" If your dream is rooted in fear, comparison, or a desire to prove your worth, it won't sustain you. It will enslave you.

Once your motives are exposed, it's time to purify. This is the soul detox where you clean the lens through which you see God, yourself, and your calling. Just like filtering water removes impurities, purifying your beliefs allows you to identify toxic narratives and exchange them for truth. Maybe you've been carrying beliefs like "I have to hustle to matter" or "God blesses me only when I perform." These aren't truths. They're traumas disguised as strategies. When you purify your beliefs, you give God space to rewrite your identity from the inside out. Through Scripture, prayer, and honesty, your mindset gets recalibrated to reflect the heart of your Designer, not the pressure of your environment or the stereotypes of your origin story.

Finally, you occupy. This is where faith becomes embodied. It's one thing to know who you are, it's another thing to walk like it. Occupying your identity means stepping boldly into your calling with spiritual authority and emotional maturity. No apologies. Imagine being given the keys to a new house but having to sleep on the floor because you never moved in. Occupy is about owning your space: Taking the meeting. Launching the brand. Saying no with clarity. Speaking up with grace. This isn't about ego, it's about alignment. You don't need more validation, you need more embodiment. Show up as the version of you that already knows that God has equipped and assigned you and is walking with you.

Optimization doesn't come from doing more, it comes from becoming more aligned. When you verify your motives, purify your beliefs, and occupy your identity, you don't just succeed, you succeed as the full version of you that was never for sale.

### Principle 5: Seek Support When Needed

Optimization does not mean isolation. God created us for community and interdependence. Galatians 6:2 tells us to carry one another's burdens. Heeding that call is a key to optimizing your life to reach your full potential. No matter how often you verify, purify, and occupy, on your own you will never see all your potential or the blind spots that keep you from reaching it. God intends for our growth to be a shared experience. We believe that specific people are assigned to our lives for this purpose. The mutual benefits related to growth, alignment, and success that come from people depositing into one another through their unique personalities and giftings create an unmatched ecosystem for optimization. Allowing them to walk in their purpose and grow just as they allow you into their growth keeps you all on a trajectory of success.

**KEVIN**

Of all the steps I took in the run-up to my Hollywood Bowl performance, the first and most important was putting together a team of believers, of dream defenders, of creative partners who knew exactly how personal and purposeful this performance was for me. My team included my creative directors, Lindsey and Craig; our musical directors, Mateo Messina and Lucas Sader; and my management team. They all understood my why behind the project and kept me on track toward it. Over the course of two and a half months, they pushed me hard so that together we could create something I never could have done on my own.

Getting support is about more than getting help. It is about being seen, understood, and guided by people who care more about your joy than about your perfection. Together, they help create a space where you can be vulnerable and they can be honest. The best teams see possibility even when you can't. The result will exceed anything you can ask for or imagine.

Everyone needs support. Everyone needs a team. Every one of us needs to move out of the realm of "me" and into the realm of "we." Optimization thrives in a community where we receive support and give it to others. Seeking support also includes seeking help from professionals when emotional barriers block your progress. Again, none of us can fulfill our life's purposes on our own. God's strength is made perfect in our weakness, and so many times the way God shows up is through others. Optimization demands the humility to admit that I cannot do this alone, that I do not have all the answers, that I need others just as they need me. James 4:6 says that God is opposed to the proud but gives grace to the humble. Support is that grace, something we all desperately need.

## When It All Comes Together

DONOVAN

I'm not really a fan of live concerts or sporting events, and living in Los Angeles, there are a lot of those. I'm more of a "lie in my hammock with my snacks and enjoy the show on my big screen" type of guy. But Kevin graciously offered me a box seat close to the stage at the Hollywood Bowl and I just could not resist. More than free tickets made me go. Several times in the months leading up to the show, Kevin had shared with me his heart's desire for this moment of divine self-expression. He never went into all the details, but he gave me just enough to make it clear that alignment with God our Creator was about to birth something I did not want to miss.

On the night of the show, I walked from the parking lot to the amphitheater with a deep excitement in my stomach. That's not like me. I'm usually Mr. Steady. But this night somehow felt different. The show started out incredibly. I'd never seen Pentatonix live, and I was impressed. Witnessing these five individuals work as a team and own the stage with the gift that God gave, for the purpose he gave, was amazing. If nothing else had come of that night, that would have been enough.

But, of course, there was more to the night, my whole reason for being there.

And then came the moment: "Kevin's Fifth." I had imagined this moment many times, but the actual experience was greater than anything I'd come up with. It wasn't just how Kevin played the cello and beatboxed, or the power of the army of cellos accompanying him along with his bandmate Matt on the drums. Nor was it strictly Lil Buck's Memphis jookin', where it looked as if gravity had decided to take a nap, or Kevin unexpectedly joining him. What made the experience unforgettable was how I could feel heaven leaning into the atmosphere, affirming the moment, the man, the music. You can't force a moment like that. It's a return on the investment of your surrender to God.

Watching "Kevin's Fifth" unfold onstage, feeling the energy from the roaring applause and the standing ovation, I knew how important this moment and this performance were for Kevin, but I also knew this moment was birthed not in his heart but in God's. God gave Kevin the "desire of the heart" to hope for this moment. I remember how proud I was of Kevin—yes, for the display, but even more for the work he did to occupy faith, occupy courage, occupy and fully embody who God ordained him to be. If I was that proud, I can only imagine how our Creator felt. Kevin had given everything he had. Afterward he told me how emotionally, spiritually, and physically spent he was. And yet I could see on his face that he was completely at peace. He had accomplished what he had set out to do, but more than that, this performance and everything leading up to it had changed Kevin and moved him closer to his ultimate goals on the trajectory of success. This performance showed the power of optimization, of alignment, and of total surrender to God. It's the same power that is available to any of us willing to step into it.

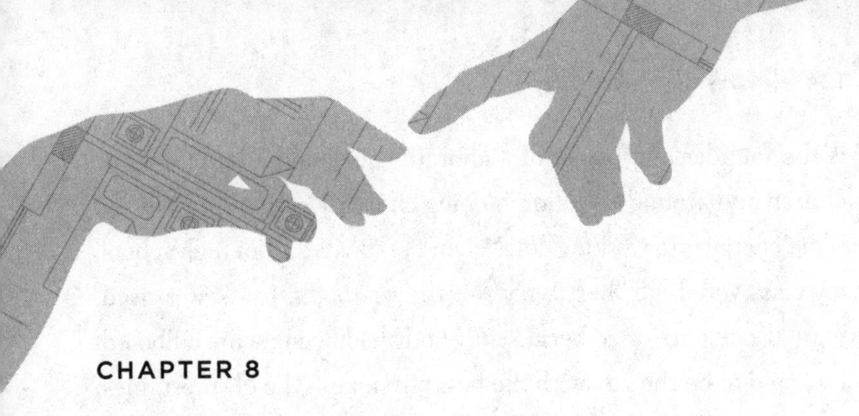

CHAPTER 8

# FOCUS ON INCREMENTAL PROGRESS

DONOVAN

When I was about ten years old, my mom bought me my first set of weights. "I don't want you to have skinny legs like your dad," she said jokingly, but I knew she was serious. None of my childhood heroes like He-Man had skinny legs, so why would I? She didn't know then that she had just awakened what turned into a lifelong love for me. Lifting weights and working out quickly became another layer on which my identity was being built. By the time I was in high school, I had moved past my first little weight set and spent so much time in the gym that it became my second church. That doesn't mean I showed up there twice a year right around Christmas and Easter. When your grandfather is the founder and pastor of a church, you spend a lot of time at church and around the church doing church-y activities. I put the same energy into working out. When I graduated from high school, my class voted me "best body" for the yearbook. I was surprised, but I also felt affirmed because my body had become my billboard. I wanted to be the guy with the best physique—the cleanest lines, the deepest cuts, the kind of body that spoke before I ever said a word. Deeper than that, my physique was all about control. At the time, I did not yet understand who I was or what I was created to be, so my body was the one thing I could shape. I thought that if I achieved the physique I wanted, it would somehow be my ticket to success, to the life I had always fantasized about.

I've grown a lot since then, especially in my understanding of my Creator and the limits of the flesh. I still work out, but it's no longer all about the aesthetics—the abs symmetry, that superhero silhouette—or the outward strength. I am developing that inner strength as someone who can handle resistance, carry weight, and still move with precision. My physical fitness now reflects that character formation—the discipline, patience, resilience, and ability to keep pushing when everything in me screams to walk away. The gym taught me to make peace with repetition and to show up even when there's no applause. Even from the beginning, when my motives were highly ego driven, as I look back, I see the gym as a metaphorical guru that showed me how to prioritize process over performance or outcome. To this day, every rep is a sermon that speaks to the potential inside me: Practice doing the hard stuff when it is not necessary so that when it is necessary, it won't break you.

The gym has taught me that there are no shortcuts to success. Working out offers growth you earn one fraction of an inch at a time. Obviously, I realize there are shortcuts for attaining the body you desire through steroids or diuretics, crash diets, even surgery. I tried the shortcuts for a season. But the one thing no one ever tells you about shortcuts, whether in building a body or building a business, is that every shortcut comes with higher taxes and hidden fees. I found that whatever profit I hoped to gain turned into a deficit that left me having to recover and rebuild in order to gain any fulfilling, sustainable enhancement. Shortcuts might get you the same look, but they do not deliver the same value. You can manufacture the image, but you cannot fabricate the internal strength, mental fortitude, supreme character, or ability to teach others that comes from staying committed to the process one step at a time. Steroids can blow you up fast, but they don't teach you patience. Diuretics can give you an overnight six-pack, but they don't give you self-control. The look always fades fast if the character behind it isn't real.

Living fully within your unique design for success begins with learning to live spiritually anchored, with integrity and self-discipline, while also enjoying the journey along the way. I've learned that success in the gym or any other area of life isn't built overnight. It's built through incremental growth—a foundational principle of success. Whatever you are working toward, the real value lies less in what you will attain and more in what you will become through the process. It is the process that shapes you. If you shortcut the process, you shortcut yourself. Remember, God is not just preparing your dream for you. He's preparing you to be ready for the dream when it comes.

More than likely, nothing you've read here is new to you. But having head knowledge about these things is different from embracing them. Even though you may understand that sustainable growth is a slow, methodical, step-by-step process, that won't stop you from hoping for and searching out a faster way. You may be tempted to acquire more than you have the capacity to manage, but that will only turn your opportunities into burdens, dampen your passion, and drain your joy; you might gain a type of success without feeling successful. Deep down, we all want to move quickly to our goal whether or not we are ready for it. Please hear this: If you're not ready for it, you won't be able to handle it when it comes.

Focusing on incremental progress—and seeing it as a good, important part of the process—requires effort, which is why we're offering the following mind shifts as well as practical application steps for each one to aid you along the way. Our goal is to help you see each step of progress as a milestone to be celebrated, honored, and fully digested. Please don't rush past these steps. They are what will pull you through to the full, true success you're seeking without your growing weary along the way.

### Mind Shift 1: Understand God's Model for Growth

The seeds of one of the largest living organisms on the planet, the giant sequoia tree, are only three to six millimeters long. (In comparison, long-grain rice is six to seven millimeters long.) But out of that small seed grows a tree that reaches nearly 300 feet tall. The largest sequoia of them all, the General Sherman tree in Sequoia National Park in California, is 275 feet tall with a circumference of more than 100 feet at its base. It weighs an estimated twelve million pounds. Although sequoias are among the fastest-growing trees on earth, it took the General Sherman tree some time to get to this size—about 2,200 years!—making it one of the oldest living things on earth as well.

What do sequoia trees have to do with success? Everything. Trees and plants follow the same divine design for growth: Seeds don't instantly turn into mature trees and immature trees do not bear fruit. The process takes time and patience. The same is true of whatever plans you may have. Seed → roots → maturity → fruit is vital for the sustainability of your success and to enhance the chances for your success to have maximum impact. Look at it this way:

- Seed: This is the vision that comes from the gravitational pull of the burdens you discover as you imagine your potential.
- Roots: These grow as you commit and recommit to the vision during the process of developing yourself to meet the requirements the vision demands of your body, mind, and emotions.
- Maturity: This growth is about *you* more than it is about whatever project you may be working on. When it comes to success, your character development is one of the main safeguards for ensuring that any success you experience will not be at the expense of your identity, morals, or

values. Proverbs 19:2 says that those who rush lose their way. Incremental growth allows you to evolve authentically, maintain alignment with your values, and become the person who can responsibly steward your dream when it manifests.

- Fruit: This comes after maturity, when you are able to step into the role of a giver, someone who doesn't just carry a gift but shares it generously. That's where fulfillment lives—not just in what you achieve but in what you give away.

This process is anathema to the instantaneous results our culture demands, which celebrates "overnight" success while ignoring the years of work it took to get there. I, Kevin, had to overcome this mindset when I started working on my debut solo album at the age of thirty-five in an industry where most new artists are in their late teens or early twenties. Comparing myself with artists like Billie Eilish and Lorde, who had hit records as teenagers, I wasn't just old, I was ancient! But when I look back at the process that began seventeen years earlier when I first started experimenting with cello-boxing—which led to my joining Pentatonix, which led to my Hollywood Bowl performance, which led to my developing my sound, my story, and my vocals for my album *Dawn of a Misfit*—I knew my first album could not have happened any other way. I had to grow to the point where that fruit could be born.

You should never be ashamed of how long your process takes. Your journey is God's way of keeping his promise to work all things together for good for those who love God and are called according to his purpose (Rom. 8:28). When you align with God, you will feel a divine gravitational pull that reveals your path, and you'll experience a type of favor in your coming and going that will give you further clarity and confidence.

Sustainable success is built on alignment, not acceleration. Incremental growth honors the process of becoming so that your success doesn't outpace your identity.

### Practical Application Steps

1. Reflect: What areas of your life are you rushing away from out of pressure or fear?
2. Journal prompt: Where do you need to honor the season you are in instead of fighting it?
3. Anchor verse: Zechariah 4:10 says, "Do not despise these small beginnings, for the Lord rejoices to see the work begin" (NLT). God gave these words to ancient Israel when the foundation of the new temple in Jerusalem was laid. The people were anxious to finish the work quickly, but God knew it was going to take years to complete.

## Mind Shift 2: Build Success in Layers, Not Leaps

Think of life like building a house. First comes the foundation. Then the framing. Next the exterior walls and the roof. After the roof and walls are in place, the electrical and plumbing go in, followed by drywall and flooring. Finally come the finishings: kitchen cabinets, appliances, bathroom fixtures, paint, light fixtures, window treatments, rugs, and furniture. There's a logic and flow to the process, with each layer dependent on what came before. If you rush the foundation to get the walls up, the house may go up fast, but the foundation will crumble. In the same way, you can't add splashes of color with paint until the interior walls are up and the drywall is finished no matter how anxious you are to get to that step. Every step prepares the way for those that come next.

The same is true of success. It is built in layers, with each stage preparing the way for whatever comes next. Yes, this is completely countercultural. It may even feel as if you're doing something wrong when you're not constantly stressing over the next level and the next and the next long before you get there, because our culture tells you you're not hungry or driven enough if you move at a slower pace. But when you lean in to this way of being by faith and fully remain in each level until you are ready to move to the next, you will discover a journey that brings greater satisfaction than the destination alone ever could. This isn't laziness, nor is it holding back. Rather, this is a patient, layered approach that will keep you from leaping into an environment that simply isn't ready yet. This is incremental growth through integration, not just acquisition.

You don't bake a cake by frosting it before it goes into the oven. The batter has to be mixed, the cake has to bake and then cool, and only then can you layer on the frosting. Success works the same way. Try to frost a half-baked cake and not only will it fall apart, it won't even taste right. Everybody wants the corner office or the big stage, but you don't get there without first learning the smaller lessons: showing up on time, handling feedback, growing in your role, building trust with people. Those layers prepare you to handle the weight of future responsibility and leadership. If you skip them, the promotion will become a pressure that collapses you instead of elevating you.

When you understand the importance of this patient, intentional growth, instead of worrying about how fast you can get to the next level, you will actually enjoy the process and be fully present within it. And you'll start to see that not only does God provide you what is needed for each day, but also he places treasures in each day to help, guide, and encourage you—like your child noticing the detailed work you're doing and telling you they are inspired by you or coming across a sermon while you're rebranding your business and finding in it a grounding verse that speaks exactly to your heart's intention for the business, clarifying and solidifying that intention so you follow it moving forward.

**KEVIN**

The layers upon which success is built are often easier to see in the rearview mirror. At least that's true for me. I've already written about how I was invited to join Pentatonix right after I graduated from Yale. Scott, Matt, Kirstin, and Avi added me as the beatboxer right before the auditions for *The Sing-Off*, which we eventually won. If my story was a fairy tale I was telling to my kids, I could add "and everyone lived happily ever after." Based on where we are today, the story pretty much feels like that, but there is far more to it.

I've also written about how I felt like a bit of a misfit in this group. Scott, Matt, and Kirstin grew up together and shared a dream of something like Pentatonix happening for them. They had basically spent their lives preparing for the group's formation and the success we've experienced. Me, not so much. It wasn't just that I hadn't given serious thought to a career in music. More, I didn't know the business like they did—the ins and outs of band life.

After my "Julie-O" video went viral, a lot of offers came my way. Of course, Pentatonix contacted me, as did *The New York Times*, who wanted an exclusive for the release of my next video. But before either of them called, a band called Gungor invited me to join them on their upcoming tour as the opening act for the David Crowder Band. Michael Gungor, who started the band along with his wife, Lisa, told me they were in a bind. Normally they traveled with a ten-plus-piece band, including strings and percussion. On this tour, however, they were limited to just the two of them. They had seen my video and thought I could fill in some of the gaps left by not having their full band. I met with them, and it felt like a match made in heaven.

When I went out on tour with Gungor, I was not thinking about layers of success or how one experience prepared me for what might lie ahead of me. What I was thinking about was how ill prepared I was for life in a touring band. For one thing, the voice of self-doubt kept ringing in my ears telling me I was not ready for this step. I had never toured before. I had never done the same show night after night in city after city. Who was I to think I could?

More than that, I did not know the basics of life in a band.

We traveled from city to city in a bus where I slept in one of the compartments built into the walls that was about the size of an open-faced coffin with only a curtain between me and everyone else. When the area is that small, you have to respect the shared space and shared air by not going number two on the bus. Let's just say I learned that lesson fast.

Onstage, my ear monitors kept falling out because I had never worked with them before. The touring crew enjoyed joking with me about it before finally helping me out. Then there was the timing and the schedule and trying to carve out the hours and hours of daily rehearsal I needed before doing shows at night.

I made so many mistakes on that tour! But Michael and Lisa and the rest of their crew extended so much grace that I got through all my missteps. They gave me a safe space to figure out the world of a professional touring musician, lessons I sorely needed for when that tour ended and I rejoined Pentatonix for the finals of *The Sing-Off.* Those lessons have served me well as a bandmate ever since.

Since that start in 2011, I've climbed up one layer after another musically, logistically, and professionally. From writing songs to producing to arranging—I started out with zero knowledge of each and slowly watched and learned and advanced one layer at a time. Honestly, I don't know that I ever felt ready for the next layer, but that did not stop me from fully occupying that space. The key, I learned, was not to be in a hurry to advance.

Each moment needs your full and undivided attention. Psalm 118:24 says, "This is the day the Lord has made. We will rejoice and be glad in it" (NLT). *This* day, today, is the day that the Lord has made available for you to occupy. That is why you must choose to rejoice in today and be glad in it. *In* it. Not through it. Not rushing past it. Only as you fully occupy it and choose to accept and make the most of this day will this day prepare you for what tomorrow will bring, one layer at a time.

### Practical Application Steps

1. Write a layered growth map: dream → vision → strategy → daily actions.
2. Celebrate micro wins. Don't wait until the big finish to validate your efforts. What win do you need to celebrate today?
3. Find an accountability partner, someone to walk in your next step with you.

## Mind Shift 3: Adopt the Mindset of a Steward, Not a Sprinter

DONOVAN

A sprinter's mindset is so focused on the finish that the only thing that matters is getting there as fast as possible. If a shortcut can help you get there quicker, you take it or lose out, because if you don't take it, someone else will. While I was an exotic dancer, I approached dancing and using my body as a vehicle with the same mindset as a sprinter, sometimes with even more abandon. My body was my bait and moneymaker. My goal was to get the audience to have some sort of internal experience as fast as possible with the fantasy I was selling, because exotic dancing is all about stage presence inviting in an audience experience that arouses specific emotions, which leads to open wallets. The sooner they were captivated, the sooner the money was thrown my way. It was a very lucrative business. But in the end I paid a price that was costlier than any benefit I might have gained.

When I finally developed the mindset of a steward, it changed how I viewed my body and my life. A steward is a caretaker of something that belongs to someone else. The Bible makes it clear that God is the ultimate owner of everything, including the dreams he gives and the lives he gives us to reach those dreams. So rather than use my body to chase an outward goal, I understood that I was to care for it and nurture it for a larger goal that would stretch over my whole life. First Corinthians 6:19–20 says, "Don't you realize that your body is the temple of the Holy Spirit, who lives in you and was given to you by God? You do not belong to yourself, for God bought you with a high price. So you must honor God with your body" (NLT). When I understood this truth, I saw myself and everything I did in a completely different light.

This life belongs to God. And so now I live to reflect that ownership over my life and use every part of my life to profit my owner. I don't need to be flashy to gain what I need. God asks only that I act faithfully. He will do the rest.

### Practical Application Steps

1. Make a list of what you already have, including your time, talent, and treasure, and ask God how you can multiply it.
2. Do a monthly check-in. What is growing slowly but surely in your life right now?

3. Put faith into action. Give something small that you have, whether it is an idea or an act of service, and trust God with its return.

As you reflect on this chapter, we invite you to consider these final practical steps:

1. Commit to improving just 1 percent of your life each day, whether it's communication, time management, or your relationship with God. Track it weekly.
2. Take five minutes at the end of each day to ask yourself, "Where did I grow today, even in a small way?" and, "How does who I say I am align with my actions?"
3. Break your big goals into smaller, character-building steps. Don't just set outcome goals (e.g., launch a business). Set integrity goals as well.

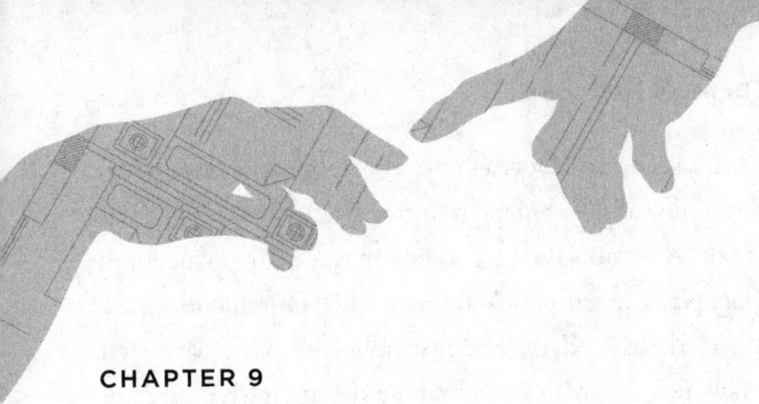

CHAPTER 9

# PRIORITIZE SABBATH BREAKS

God took the first Sabbath break. Genesis 2:1–3 says, "So the creation of the heavens and the earth and everything in them was completed. On the seventh day God had finished his work of creation, so he rested from all his work. And God blessed the seventh day and declared it holy, because it was the day when he rested from all his work of creation" (NLT).

God did not rest because he was tired. Since God is God, he never tires. Nor was a day of rest God's reward to himself for a job well done. He deserved it, though, after looking over all he had created and declaring it very good. But a day of rest—*Shabbat* in Hebrew, from which we derive the English word "Sabbath"—is not given simply as a reward for all our hard work through the week. Rather, when God set aside the seventh day as holy, he was inserting the principle of divine rest into the natural flow of all of creation.

Sabbath may be the fourth out of the Ten Commandments, but it's not some rule God made to torment us. He established it as a gift to us. As Jesus said, "The Sabbath was made to meet the needs of people, and not people to meet the requirements of the Sabbath" (Mark 2:27 NLT). The principle is so basic. We need a day of holy rest, a day to recalibrate, a day to, in the words of Psalm 46:10, be still and know that he is God. Taking Sabbath is an act of faith, perhaps the first act of faith any person ever takes. Exodus 20:9–10 puts it like this: "You have six days each week for your ordinary work, but the seventh day is a Sabbath day of rest dedicated to the Lord your God" (NLT). God was demonstrating that rest is not a break from productivity but a spiritual territory of time where he is the center instead of your work. By setting aside one full day to cease from all our activities and focus on God, we are in effect declaring that the Lord is the real source of our strength. Sabbath is meant to be a day when we humble ourselves, a day when we remember that our real worth is tied not to our output but to our relationship with God. This day recenters our identity in divine purpose rather than in our performance. It is a sacred day of rest we must protect at all costs.

---

**DONOVAN**

In the grand scheme of things, one day a week to cease our ordinary work and dedicate it to God is not a huge ask. But in a world that tells us that the only way to succeed is to work 24/7/365, stopping for even a couple of hours to go to church or do some "faith" activity feels like a big sacrifice. The very fact that a weekly Sabbath break, an idea as old as time itself, feels radical is in itself a revelation of our need for Sabbath. Feeling like my work is too important to pause for a day shows how out of alignment my understanding of work is. This attitude also reveals an overinflated view of oneself and a deep-seated belief that I am so central to my success that if I stopped even for a day, all would fall apart. Deuteronomy 8:18 reminds us that it is God who gives us the ability to acquire wealth. This means that all our talents and abilities are gifts from God for us to develop and use. A Sabbath day of rest is our way of honoring that aspect of God's activity and giving him thanks for it. It acknowledges that he is our source, not ourselves.

I have found no other replacement for a Sabbath break from work. Setting aside what my mind believes I cannot afford to set aside has become the place where I meet the author and giver of life and success. In this place of meeting, the verify, purify, occupy exercise becomes a divine conversation. I am not just checking myself. I am living out the prayer of Psalm 139:23–24 (NLT):

> Search me, O God, and know my heart;
> test me and know my anxious thoughts.
> Point out anything in me that offends you,
> and lead me along the path of everlasting life.

Going into a day of rest with this expectation transforms it from a day off to a day of recalibration with God.

I did not grow up understanding the purpose of the Sabbath

day even though I was at my grandfather's church all the time. Church days were workdays for me. Sunday services started at 8:00 a.m. and usually went until around 2:00 p.m., with another service in the evening. I helped count money, clean up the sanctuary, clear the parking lot, and basically do whatever needed to be done to get the building ready for the evening service. Sometimes we even had staff meetings between services. Sunday may have been the Lord's Day, but it was anything but a Sabbath rest for me. Sometimes it's hard to keep your focus on God when you have to clean a toilet while wearing your Sunday-best suit.

It wasn't until my days as a dancer that I started keeping a real Sabbath. My girlfriend at that time, who was also a dancer, was a Seventh-day Adventist, and she introduced me to the idea. I know the idea of a couple of strippers observing a religious Sabbath day sounds like a huge contradiction. How can someone dance half naked in a club every night of the week, then turn around and honor a day as God's holy day of rest? It may have been a contradiction, but that was exactly what God used to unravel my performance-based identity.

At first, keeping the Sabbath with my girlfriend was nothing more than a relationship checkbox. But over time it went from a checkbox to something I knew I needed. I learned the value of sitting quietly listening to preaching and worship music and hearing testimonies that reminded me of God's Word and character. In the beginning I felt I could afford to give only a half day for a Sabbath. Rather than feel guilty, I accepted God's grace that whatever I could give at the start was enough. Those Sabbath breaks to focus on God eventually led me to a place where I had the faith, conviction, and courage to leave the club. My life changed in ways I never foresaw when I started setting aside a day each week to enhance my proximity to God and his will for my life. And I've learned that there is no real success without it.

**KEVIN**

I grew up in the Seventh-day Adventist Church, which sets aside sunset Friday to sunset Saturday as a Sabbath to the Lord, so I never knew a time without a Sabbath break. My mom grew up Seventh-day Adventist in Grenada, and Caribbean Seventh-day Adventists are intense about everything! As a kid, I understood that Sabbath was important, but that didn't keep me from being bored and feeling a little left out because I didn't get to watch all the cool Saturday-morning cartoons like the other kids did. As I understood it, God wanted our time even if it was at the same time as *Garfield and Friends*. Instead, I'd get up really early and watch Christian music videos and cartoons like *Superbook* and *The Flying House* on the Christian channels.

When I became an adult and worked through my own beliefs and convictions, I learned to appreciate the Sabbath as a day date with God, similar to a day date with my wife when we leave the kids with grandparents and go out simply to enjoy being together. My focus on the Sabbath is time with him. This isn't something I have to do to make God like me. God already loves me. When I give him that time, I feel his love. Setting aside time for Sabbath does not mean sitting in a small room meditating on Bible verses. Instead, it can look like worshiping as a family or going out into the beauty of nature surrounded by God's creativity. The point is to disconnect from work and home-improvement projects and bills to focus on the goodness of God. All the pressures and worries and stress I accumulate through the week look different in his presence. I come away with a sense of rejuvenation in my mind, body, and spirit that I cannot get any other way. I get to see things from an eternal perspective rather than from my normal, everyday, ephemeral perspective. As a result, the Sabbath breaks the negative-feedback loops and gives me a new sense of connection with God and his purpose for me.

Prioritizing Sabbath rest is an act of faith that tells God, "I trust you to hold what I've been trying to control." The benefits we've experienced by prioritizing weekly Sabbath breaks have enhanced our ability to succeed beyond what we ever imagined. Open up to the idea of giving that one day a week to rest and reflection and see whether you experience these same benefits in your own life.

### 1. Prioritizing Sabbath Breaks Frees You from Grind Mode to Walk in a Grace Rhythm

KEVIN

When I left home to finish high school at Andover and later attend Yale, my mom and dad weren't there to remind me to observe the Sabbath. None of my professors ever asked, "Did you keep the Sabbath this week?" Instead they were asking, "Did you finish the assignment?" and, "Are you ready for the test?" and "How do you plan to defend this thesis?" The academic demands felt so relentless that I started making quiet compromises. I didn't do Sabbath breaks while in school. Instead, I told myself that God understands and he knows my heart, while deep down inside one question kept gnawing at me: "Do I still believe this matters?"

After I graduated from college and joined Pentatonix, I discovered a whole new level of pressure. Music had always been a passion, something I did only for fun. Now it was my profession. On top of that, I was one of five in the group, and we all depended on one another not just to make music but for our livelihood. All five of us were determined to make our group succeed, which meant grind mode 24/7. We took whatever gigs we could and never stopped working, even if those gigs occurred during what was supposed to be my Sabbath. Success meant grabbing opportunities when they presented themselves. We needed the exposure as a band and we needed the money to pay the bills. Suddenly the Sabbath wasn't an esoteric theological question but a career decision. If I could not perform on Friday nights, the rest of the band would find a beatboxer who could.

To be honest, I found it easier and easier to justify ignoring the Sabbath. Whenever a Friday night or daytime Saturday gig came up, it wasn't worth it to be the one who made things more difficult for the other members of the band. After all, we were gaining momentum. I didn't want to disrupt it. It's a lot easier to build on momentum than to try to start over from a dead start. Everyone knows that. We might never get these opportunities again.

At least that's what I told myself, even though my compromises were eating me up inside.

I might have kept on justifying blowing off Sabbath breaks forever if not for my sister, who was staying with me in Los Angeles during the summer of 2012. She could see my internal conflict. It was written all over my face. Finally, she couldn't take it any longer. In the courtyard of my apartment complex, she looked at me and said, "Kevin, this career isn't yours. God gave you all of this. You know beyond the shadow of a doubt that he's the one who brought you here. You didn't get here by yourself. So if God gave you this life and career, then you have to honor him with it."

I stood there quiet and convicted. Then she said words that became the turning point of my story: "God will make a way for you to keep the Sabbath in this band. And if it's not the way, then he'll make another way for you, and that's okay. God's way is more important than man's."

I knew she was right, but I still struggled to do what I needed to do. Did I really believe that God could sustain my career if I honored him in a way that seemed foolish to everyone else? That forced me to ask even deeper questions: What did success mean to me? Was success doing things the way I imagined others wanted me to, or was it doing things God's way? How would Sabbath rest benefit me? Moreover, could I trust God with my career and life? Honestly, in that moment, I didn't know the answers. But one thing I did know: My relationship with God and the convictions upon which it was based meant more to me than anything else, no matter the cost.

I opened up to my bandmates at our next meeting. I started off by apologizing for not bringing up this issue earlier simply because I was scared of how they'd react, but I knew it was only fair to be honest and up-front with them if I was going to be their bandmate. I went on to explain how throughout my life I had always observed the Sabbath from sunset Friday to sunset Saturday to spend time with God. "This is very important to me and I believe I need to do this now even as a part of the band." You can imagine the looks on their faces as they listened to what I said. Dumbfounded. Confused. Hurt. Angry. Completely blindsided. Even Avi, our bass voice at the time and one of my closest friends, who grew up a Messianic Jew, didn't get it. Someone else jumped in with the question on everyone's mind: "So how are we supposed to earn a living if we can't do Friday-night shows?" I didn't have the answer, but I knew I had to hold to my convictions. I ended with telling the band one of the hardest things I could offer: If we could not find a way to make this work, I would help them find another beatboxer to replace me.

I'm glad they decided to stick with me, but it wasn't easy for any of us in the beginning. A gig would come up during Sabbath, and I could see the deflated emotion in my bandmates. It felt like I constantly let them down because of my special "issue," and so the guilt and shame would engulf me, along with a whole lot of anxiety: *I made a mistake. I messed up. I'm one gig away from getting kicked out.* But that wasn't true. With time, my friends and I discovered how to show one another grace, and we learned to create win-win situations for everyone. I made sure to work right up to the beginning of my Sabbath break. I also made sure I worked hard for the band's success the six days I was available.

I did sound checks earlier in the day or anything else the band needed. If they needed to do a show or appear on a red carpet or do a recording session without me, I gave them my full support. Sabbath was my conviction, not theirs, so I never expected them to stop working on Friday nights or Saturdays.

This is what a rhythm of grace looks like. Success isn't about nonstop effort. It's about aligned energy. Sabbath breaks are a necessary part of the process. They give you permission to slow down, listen to your internal compass, and feel God breathe into your life, your career, your motivations. They center you so that you're not driven by external pressures. When you're spiritually filled up, you can easily give the other six days your overflow. Yes, you'll see great results with this rhythm of grace, but beyond those results, this rhythm ensures a sustainable momentum, enhancing your effectiveness while reducing the dangers of burnout. Ultimately, living into your convictions and allowing God to speak into what you're doing will multiply the impact of your efforts!

### 2. Prioritizing Sabbath Breaks Frees You from Proving Your Worth to Living from Your Worth

DONOVAN

After getting rejected by an acting and modeling agency—something I had staked so much of my self-worth on—I felt lost and angry. That rejection didn't just bruise my ego. It cracked open a part of me that I had carefully kept hidden: my insecurities, my need for validation, and the little boy inside me who struggled with not being liked by everyone—an issue that was born during my sixth-grade year of middle school when a girl in eighth grade didn't want to be my girlfriend. I took that as rejection, made it painfully personal, and allowed it to fracture my hope when it came to social acceptance instead of letting it be an isolated event. Dancing in the club filled that need for acceptance, if only for as long as I was onstage. I loved being seen, desired, and applauded. At the time, that external validation felt like enough.

Then entered the Sabbath. Each week as I paused to rest and focus on God, I was unknowingly participating in a detox, a divine interruption of everything I thought defined me. The process started slowly. The first cracks in my performance facade came as I watched my girlfriend's intentionality and sincerity on our Sabbaths together. It was almost as though an unveiled version of her appeared. That made me wonder whether there was an unveiled version of me as well. I was so deep in character on the club stage that that persona had started to define me off the stage too. Did I dare look below the surface? As a life coach I now understand that the right question can start transformational conversations when asked in a safe or sacred environment. My Sabbath breaks gave me that space. Slowly I began to see the difference between the man I had become and the man God designed me to be. I stopped seeing the Sabbath as a day off and started seeing it as a mirror that God was using to show me who I really was and, just as important, who I wasn't.

When I was growing up, my mother used to tell me over and over, "Donovan, you are energy wrapped in flesh." What was inside me was where my true life and identity lay. In the quiet of my Sabbath day when I was listening for the voice of God, I remembered her words. And I realized I wasn't just a body to be displayed. I was a vessel designed to carry freedom, light, and truth into the world. But I wasn't living into that truth. Instead I had settled for a life onstage that was completely misaligned with the destiny God had written over me. When I first went up on the club stage, I was searching for validation, for worth, because I believed I had something to prove. But there in the quiet, sitting in the presence of God for one entire day a week, giving him my undivided attention, I realized, through a subtle feeling of knowing that arose in my spirit, that I was already seen and approved by God. Instead of striving for attention, I started listening for his intention.

It took two years, but I finally reached the place where I knew a drastic change was needed. I will never forget that day, April 24, 2004. A day I chose to rest and Sabbath in God. I was sitting on the edge of my bed praying when I heard God say, "Quit." God and I had already had similar conversations a few times before in which I always came back with some rebuttal. But not this time. I simply said, "Okay." The strength to make that decision came not from me but from consistently stepping into the rest and recovery of God's presence.

My Sabbath break has remained to this day. The more I've honored the Sabbath, the more I've realized no one's worth is tied to performance but is anchored in God's divine purpose for each one of us. You need a Sabbath break. It will give you a significant amount of time for weekly stillness when you can reconnect with the core of who you were made to be. That truth can be hard to hold on to while surrounded by hustle culture or wrestling with the need for consistent validation. But when you move from trying to prove your worth to living out of your intrinsic worth as a child of God, you will be truly liberated.

### 3. Prioritizing Sabbath Breaks Takes You from Doing for God to Being with God

KEVIN

In 2021, Donovan and I started a podcast we named *Imagine Faith Talk*. A podcast had never been on our radar until our good friend Kor asked us to pray about doing one. Once we felt certain God was in this, we were all in. We spent months preparing for the podcast launch, the three of us meeting regularly to refine our message and plan our format. Finally, in April 2022, we recorded our first episode: "You Don't Have to Sell Your Soul to Obtain Your Dreams." Sort of sounds like this book, huh?

Neither of us expected to have so much fun doing the podcast. We loved it. As with this book, we were fascinated to flesh out in real-world terms what success means from a heavenly perspective. And recording the podcast felt like getting to spend more time in God's presence together. Because of everyone's work obligations, we often recorded episodes on Saturdays when everyone was available. It was the perfect day for us to do ministry together.

My wife was very supportive of what Donovan, Kor, and I were doing, even though it pulled even more time out of my schedule on top of all the time I was away with Pentatonix and my solo projects. Recording the podcast on Saturday started out as an occasional thing but soon turned into *the* day we could do it. When I told my wife, Leigh, that I would not be available for parts of Sabbath, her look told me everything I needed to know. Rather than listen to what my eyes were telling me, I decided to do the classic man thing and explain why Saturday was the only day we could do the podcast. She did not argue. Instead, she simply said, "I understand, but I really miss you and our Saturdays that are all about us being with God as a family."

Wow. After my wife responded, my first thought was, *What kind of husband and father am I if I neglect such a crucial time with my family in the name of doing the Lord's work?* I know lots of pastors who have anything but a restful Lord's Day because it is their biggest workday of the week. But most also take another day of the week off as their Sabbath rest with their family. I was not doing that now, and as a result I was the one missing out. I immediately thought about the New Testament story of two sisters, Martha and Mary, in Luke 10:38–42. When Jesus came to their house, Martha spent all her time running around preparing food and trying to make everything perfect. Mary sat at Jesus' feet and listened. This made Martha mad. What made her sister think she didn't have to share in the work when there was such an important guest in their home? She even complained to Jesus about Mary. But Jesus gently rebuked Martha, saying, "My dear Martha, you are worried and upset over all these details! There is only one thing worth being concerned about. Mary has discovered it, and it will not be taken away from her" (vv. 41–42 NLT). I had forgotten the only thing worth being concerned about. Yes, the work on our podcast was important. It really is the Lord's work. But that didn't mean we couldn't do it on another day. I knew I had to talk to Donovan and Kor. They graciously agreed to find another time.

### So Where Do We Begin?

When God calls us to Sabbath, he isn't just giving a religious rule, he's giving us a repair prescription. Modern neuroscience affirms that extended, uninterrupted downtime is essential for optimal brain repair and creativity. Research on the brain's default mode network—a set of regions active when the mind is at rest—shows that these circuits are critical for self-reflection, problem-solving, and creative insight.[4] When we stop forcing productivity, the brain begins to reorganize, restore, and generate new connections.

While quick breaks and naps have value, they don't compare to the deeper renewal found in prolonged rest. From my own experience, I've learned that practicing a full twenty-four-hour Sabbath provides the kind of mental detachment and adrenal replenishment that prepares me for the week ahead. Science helps us understand how the brain repairs itself during rest, but Scripture reminds us that rest is not optional, it's God's design for sustainable living. A full Sabbath day, then, benefits us on multiple levels:

- Spiritually: It trains us to surrender control, proving that the world doesn't fall apart when we stop.
- Mentally: It forces the brain into deep recalibration instead of shallow "mental breaks."

- Physically: It aligns us with our natural repair cycles, allowing muscles to rebuild, cells to detoxify, hormones to rebalance, and the nervous system to reset.
- Biochemically: It flushes stress chemicals and restores energy reserves.

You can't fully reset a system by hitting pause for only an hour. God designed the Sabbath as a full reset button, which means you need to give it your time and attention.

### 1. Block It Out Before You Hijack It

- Why: If you don't schedule your Sabbath twenty-four hours in advance, life will hijack it.
- How: Put it on your calendar as "Sacred Time—No Reschedule." Tell friends and family you'll be unavailable for work-related things.
- Biblical anchor: "Remember the Sabbath day by keeping it holy" (Ex. 20:8). Holiness is about setting apart—in this case, setting apart your time.

### 2. Remove the Work Hooks

- Why: Sabbath isn't just about not working, it's also about not *thinking* about work.
- How: Before Sabbath begins, write down lingering tasks, emails, and mental to-dos in a notebook. Promise yourself you'll return to them after your twenty-four hours.
- Biblical anchor: God rested "from all his work" (Gen.

2:2). Not some—all. This is a full mental and physical disengagement.

### 3. Practice Soul Pleasure, Not Just Self-Care

- Why: The Sabbath is for delighting in God, not just for catching up on sleep or Netflix.
- How: Choose activities that reconnect you with God and with life, such as walks in nature, worship music, family meals, prayer journaling.
- Biblical anchor: Isaiah 58:13–14 promises us joy and strength when we call the Sabbath a delight.

## For Someone Who's Been Keeping Sabbath and Wants to Enhance It

### 1. Upgrade from Resting *From* to Resting *For*

- Why: Many people stop at "no work" and never enter into "spiritual renewal."
- How: Curate a Sabbath theme each week (e.g., gratitude, listening, celebration). Let your prayers, reading, and even meals reflect it.
- Biblical anchor: Jesus said, "The Sabbath was made for man" (Mark 2:27). It's a gift meant to grow you, not just to pause you.

### 2. Anchor Your Sabbath with a Ritual Start and Finish

- Why: Rituals train the brain to recognize transitions in consciousness.

- How: Light a candle, pray aloud, sing a song at the beginning. At the end, share a blessing, write a gratitude note, or have a symbolic meal to close your Sabbath.
- Biblical anchor: In Genesis 1, God defines each day with "there was evening, and there was morning," marking the transition.

### 3. Make Space for God's Interruptions

- Why: Sometimes God wants to fill your Sabbath with something unexpected: a conversation, a revelation, an insight you didn't plan.
- How: Leave part of your day unplanned. Resist the urge to structure every hour. Let God write in the margins.
- Biblical anchor: Jesus often disrupted Sabbath norms to heal or teach (Luke 13:10–17), showing that the Spirit moves in flexibility.

Success isn't about spiritual performance. It's about divine partnership. We don't prioritize Sabbath breaks to earn God's favor or to convince him that he should bless all our endeavors. We observe Sabbath to spend time in God's presence. As would any loving father, that's all he really wants from us.

CHAPTER 10

# TRUST IN GOD'S UNCONDITIONAL LOVE FOR YOU

KEVIN

I have certainly struggled in the past with my motives in my artistic pursuits. Even as a member of Pentatonix with all our success, I still carried an underlying sense of needing to prove my worth. Not only did I grow up believing I needed to do something meaningful with my life, but as a graduate of Yale I felt an obligation to do something notable, something worthy, something befitting a graduate of one of the most prestigious universities in the world. I'd be embarrassed if I didn't. After all, Yale alumni include five past United States presidents, three of the nine current members of the Supreme Court, and sixty-five Nobel Prize winners! And I'm just a beatboxer. Given that illustrious company, I believed I needed to always push myself to learn and grow and improve not only in music but in every aspect of my life to show that I am worthy to sit among these peers.

I might still be on that treadmill if it weren't for April 3, 2021. That was the day I became a father. When I held my baby girl for the first time, I was awestruck by how deeply I loved her even though she had never done a thing. As an infant, all she could do was nurse and poop and pee and sleep when we wanted her to stay awake, and stay awake when we needed her to sleep. But none of that mattered. Simply her existence as my daughter made me love her more each day. Today she's a bright-eyed four-year-old. Life with a small child is so much fun because everything in the world is new to her. She still can't cook or write an award-winning speech or make money or contribute to the overall needs of our household in any way. But she doesn't need to. She doesn't have to do a single thing to earn my love. She already has it and always will.

I think that is how God sees all of us. When the Bible calls him our heavenly Father, it isn't some empty religious term. Instead, it reveals how our Creator feels about us, his children. He loves us unconditionally, and nothing can separate us from his love. When this truth that I had heard and thought I understood all my life finally started to sink in, I stopped striving and started serving. I stopped expressing my artistry in the hope of proving I was enough. Instead, I was creating because I already was enough.

That is why trusting in God's unconditional love for you is a crucial step in your journey to success. In a day and age filled with so much fear and hate and division—some of it, unfortunately, in God's name—the simple message that God loves us unconditionally is too easily misunderstood. There are those out there who want us to think that God loves some people more than others and even despises some groups altogether. Nothing could be farther from the truth. The Bible says that God is love and that he loves the entire world. This means you are fully known, fully seen, and fully embraced by God not because of what you do but because of who you are and whose you are. It's the kind of love that doesn't wait for you to get it together, clean yourself up, or perform for approval. It's love that precedes your productivity, outlives your failures, and remains even when your faith is inconsistent.

Knowing about God's love and actually living within it can feel worlds apart. We know it's a lot to digest, so we're sharing something we've discovered: three core truths that help us understand the depth of God's love and how it transforms all our pursuits.

### 1. God's Love Is the Foundation, Not the Finish Line

DONOVAN

In ontology, we say, "You don't do to become. You be, then do." When I was an exotic dancer, I had it backward. My grind for attention was really a cry for affection. Once I encountered the unconditional love of God, though, I stopped performing for love and started expressing from love. That's the shift that God's love makes. It reorders your ontology by giving you a new way of being that no amount of applause can give and no failure can take away.

When I say that God's love found me in the middle of a strip-club hustle, I'm not speaking metaphorically. His love found me while I was standing under flashing lights, dripping with sweat and ego, while my soul was quietly suffocating. And the wild thing? I didn't even know I was lost. I was addicted to the high of being seen, but I was blind to the fact that I'd made a habit of abandoning myself.

But that's what unconditional love does. It interrupts your performance with presence. It walks into your darkest place with piercing light, not to judge but to reveal.

God's love revealed to me that I wasn't broken, I was misaligned.

I wasn't empty, I was pouring into the wrong system.

I wasn't worthless, I was misled, unable to hear the truth loud enough to drown out the lies I'd been dancing to.

God didn't wait for me to clean up to call me out. He loved me while I was still grinding, still pretending, still numb. That love gave me permission to be, not impress. To breathe, not strive. From that place of being loved, I started learning how to love myself not from ego but from essence.

Now when I coach creatives, leaders, and visionaries, I don't ask them what they do. I ask, "Who are you when you're not doing?" That's where transformation begins. That's where the lies lose their grip. That's where success stops being a mask and starts becoming a manifestation.

That's what the love of God did for me. It didn't just pull me out of the strip club. It pulled me back into myself.

This is what we mean when we say God's love is the

foundation, not the finish line. It is not a prize we win but the rock on which we perform. Trying to win God's love through success is like trying to fill a river with a bucket. You can't create the source. You're supposed to draw from it. First John 4:19 says, "We love because he first loved us." That's the order. God loves us, and whatever we do from love is now the overflow of his love. Success isn't the pathway to love; being led by his love is the pathway to success. God's love makes us worthy to enter any space that his grace opens for us. And he will always ensure the readiness of the one who is submitted to and aligned with his will.

### 2. When You Are Loved, You Don't Have to Compromise

When you trust in God's unconditional love, it sets you free to pursue success without selling your soul. You're no longer defined by whether you succeed or fail. You're defined by God's love for you. His love is like a safety harness while you climb up the face of El Capitan in Yosemite National Park. You can scale new heights without fear of falling because you are already secured. That's the thing about unconditional love. It doesn't just heal you. It anchors you. First Corinthians 6:20 tells us that we were bought by God at a price. That's the source of our freedom. When you know that the creator of the universe calls you worthy before you lift a finger, you are free to soar.

The anchor of love allows you to stay grounded in your identity without compromising your core values. Compromise is the currency of those who haven't accepted their worth. It's the currency of fear, of telling yourself you are less than, that the only way you can succeed is by becoming who others think you need to be. But when your worth is rooted in God's eternal yes, you build your life from his. We've walked into high-stakes boardrooms and creative spaces where the temptation to dilute truth for opportunity was real. But love—real love—makes you immovable. You realize, "If I have to lose myself to win here, then I've already lost."

Herein lies the real transformative power of unconditional love. When you live from a place of trust in God's unconditional love for you, you stop attracting situations that demand your compromise and start creating ecosystems that reflect your convictions. That's not arrogance. That's fearless alignment. That's liberation. And that's what we call living out your design for success—no masks, no mimicry, no moral debt. Just you, grounded in God, creating from truth without compromise born of fear.

Fear not only robs you of your authentic self but also sabotages creativity. Divine creativity can flow only from a regulated nervous system, which comes through a feeling of safety: of being seen, cared for, protected. Fear throws the entire system off balance by eliciting one of three reactions: fight, flight, or freeze. It's impossible to live out your divine purpose in any one of these modes. First John 4:18 reminds us that "love has no fear, because perfect love expels all fear. If we are afraid, it is for fear of punishment, and this shows that we have not fully experienced his perfect love" (NLT). When we fully experience God's perfect love, we are brought into psychological safety, which prompts the release of the potential he put inside us. God's unconditional love then sets the environment for you to be able to invest creatively so that you may experience any type of success. When you're living in this love, the word *failure* loses its power.

### 3. Love Fuels Legacy

**KEVIN**

When I was fresh out of college and new to Pentatonix, I thought that winning a Grammy would be a legacy maker, the kind of achievement that screams greatness and impact. Don't get me wrong—I still believe our three Grammy awards are an incredible honor, and I'd be lying if I said they were unimportant. But as I've grown in my understanding of the love of God, I realize that the point of my life and career is not winning awards or gaining fame. Far more important than being recognized is sharing the love of God through who I am and letting the Holy Spirit use me to show people who they really are in Christ. That was my goal when I started working on my first full-length solo album.

Being a misfit myself, I recognize so many other people out there who feel misunderstood and unseen. My first album, *Dawn of a Misfit,* is my letter of love to them to let them know they are seen and valued. I wrote the songs to help others see that their uniqueness *is* their superpower. It has certainly connected. Since my album's release, fans have told me how my music has been a source of healing. Kids who never thought classical music was cool now love it. Parents have told me how their nonverbal children smile and light up when they hear my songs. That's priceless! The same is true through my music in Pentatonix. I've met people at our VIP experience who have told me how they found the strength to keep living because of our music. This is where real impact lies: in serving others through my art. I close my eyes before I work and I visualize those people coming to my concert, screaming and cheering, knowing that the frequency that God gave me to share is resonating with a specific listener. It has taken a long time of deep self-work to realize that my identity is not in being the most famous musician or being in the most famous band. Those things don't drive me today. I now have a righteous ambition driven by the question, "How can I be the greatest servant I can be?" As I've seen with Jesus and even people I've worked with like Ms. Rachel (my son Christian's favorite YouTube star), that kind of service changes lives.

This is the legacy I want to leave, not only for fans but especially for my children. I want them to remember their dad not as a musician or a Grammy winner but as someone who lived out his God-given identity in love, service, and joy. Galatians 5:6 says the only thing that matters is faith expressing itself through love. In our race to achieve more and more, these words are easy to ignore. But here's the truth: Achievement is like a spark. Love is a fire. A spark flashes and then is gone, but a fire gives long-lasting warmth. The difference is love. As you trust in God's unconditional love for you, it will flow out of you, and your goal will shift from short-term success to long-term impact. Instead of measuring success by trophies, measure it by the transformation love always brings.

### From Idea to Daily Reality

While on his deathbed, Heinriche Heine, a German poet and journalist, was visited by a priest. Knowing Heine was about to pass into eternity, the priest asked Heine if he was worried about being forgiven for his sins. "Of course, God will forgive me, that's his job," Heine replied. Whether he meant his response to be cynical or hopeful, Heine's famous last words reflect how many people understand the love of God. Of course God loves and of course he forgives. He's God. That's what he's supposed to do. This idea, however, is not biblical. God's love is not something to take for granted but a reality into which we are invited. Romans 5:8 tells us that God demonstrated his great love for us by sending Christ to die for us even though we had done nothing to earn his love. Romans goes on to tell us that through Jesus we can have a new relationship in which we are friends with God. The words used there describe a closeness and intimacy that reveal a God who is very different from the distant and angry entity many think of when they think of God. That's why this chapter doesn't call you to *believe* in God's unconditional love but calls you to *trust* in God's unconditional love for *you*. While this may be a new concept for many, we have discovered some basic, practical, daily steps you can take to enter God's love in a very real way.

### 1. Practice Self-Acceptance as the Starting Point of Transformation

Whether or not you are a believer, the truth that you are already deeply loved before you do or perfect anything creates the safety needed for you to stop performing and start transforming. When we no longer fear rejection, we can face truth, and truth sets us free. But many struggle not with the idea that God loves the world but with thinking that God could love them individually.

The truth is, you cannot become who you truly are until you accept who you currently are. God accepts you. Now you have to accept yourself through a daily practice we call name, normalize, nurture.

- *Name*: Do a morning check in which you look in the mirror and name what you feel without judgment. For example, you may say, "I feel insecure about that meeting today." As you do, remind yourself that the emotions you feel do not disqualify you. Whether or not you feel it, you are still worthy to walk into that room because God loves you.
- *Normalize* your humanity: Look yourself in the eye and say, "Being human means I'm always becoming. I don't have to be perfect to be purposeful today."
- *Nurture* with truth or affirmation: For Christians, remember the truth that even when you were broken, God chose you. For all of us, remind yourself, "I am not my feelings. I am the one who observes and chooses how to respond."
- Keep a journal in which you track your identity wins, those moments when you responded from love instead of fear or performance.

Name, normalize, nurture is more than a series of self-reminders. These practices have the power to free you from perfectionism and shame-based striving while creating space for honest self-inventory and growth. This is also a powerful step toward healing false identities and replacing them with integrated being. Remember, a plant does not grow by hating its seed stage.

It flourishes because the gardener sees its potential from the beginning. God is our gardener, and his love sees not our flaws and failures but the greatness inside each one of us waiting to be unleashed.

### 2. Rewrite Your Fear Narrative with the Truth of Love

First John 4:18 tells us that God's perfect love drives out all fear, and ontology asserts that fear is a breakdown in being that stems from separation—real or perceived—from love, safety, or worth. But when you are fully seen and still fully loved, you no longer need to fear failure, criticism, or rejection. Whether you call it divine love or radical acceptance, trusting in unconditional love activates courage and healthy risk-taking. In our next exercise, which we call "catch, challenge, choose," we encourage you to use the awareness of being unconditionally loved as a way to neutralize fear:

- *Catch* the fear thought. Notice the voice of fear in real time. When you find yourself saying something like, "If I try this and fail, I will lose respect or opportunities," recognize it and call it out.
- *Challenge* the fear thought with love-based logic. Ask yourself, "Would someone who believes they are already enough be afraid of this?" Believers in Jesus can go a step farther and say, "God's love already covers me—win or lose."
- *Choose* a braver action, no matter how small it may be. Face your fear, be grounded in love, and take action. Send the email. Speak up in the meeting. Try the new thing.

Create a bravery tracker note in your phone to make a note of every time you act in love over fear. You will then be able to see your confidence compounding over time.

Catch, challenge, choose will increase your creative risk-taking and bold decision-making by regulating your nervous system, allowing you to transform anxiety into action. As when a child falls into her parent's arms knowing he will catch her when she jumps, God's love will empower you to take the jump while you keep your identity anchored in the love of God rather than outcomes or applause.

### 3. Anchor Your Excellence in Worth, Not Worry

The ontological principle of "You don't do to become; you be, then do" reminds us that being always precedes doing. When you are grounded in your inherent value, your actions flow from peace, not pressure. Our value comes from God's unconditional love. It is a sustainable source of excellence because it removes the need to perform to prove. When our identity is rooted in essence, not effort, we discover a peace that will carry us through our day. To remind ourselves daily of these truths, we have an exercise we call "Work from rest, not worry."

- Start the day in stillness. Breathe deeply and declare, "I am not what I produce. I am who I am." For the believer, you can add, "I abide in Christ, and fruit will come in season."
- Before any major task, stop and ask yourself, "Am I doing this to be seen or because I've seen who I am?"

- Add a block of time to your Sabbath ritual when you focus on replenishing, not performing. Remind yourself that value precedes value creation. Tell yourself, "I give what I expect from others." Include reading and meditating on Matthew 6, where Jesus declares, "Look at the lilies of the field and how they grow. They don't work or make their clothing, yet Solomon in all his glory was not dressed as beautifully as they are. And if God cares so wonderfully for wildflowers that are here today and thrown into the fire tomorrow, he will certainly care for you. Why do you have so little faith?" (vv. 28–30 NLT). The last line is simply asking, Do you believe this or not? If you do, what difference has it made this past week, and what changes does it prompt you to make next week?

A cherry tree doesn't force itself to bear fruit. A grapevine cannot will itself to produce grapes before their season. Plants flourish by abiding, being nourished, then allowing fruit to come naturally. When we abide in God's love and allow it to nourish our souls, fruit and productivity will flow at just the right time.

CHAPTER 11

# HOLD ON THROUGH THE PLOT TWISTS

> **Plot twist** | ˈplä(t) ˌtwist | noun | an unexpected development in a book, film, television program, etc.: *I won't give away the big plot twist.*

No. *I* am your father" is one of the greatest plot twists of all time. Even without naming the movie, we all recognize it. Those five words changed cinema forever. This plot twist was an unexpected development not just in a single movie but for an entire franchise. For the hero—the embodiment of everything good in the series—those five words turn his world upside down. Suddenly he is not who he has always believed he was. He grew up hearing stories of how his father had died defending truth. The truth is that his father is not only alive but the very definition of evil.

The audience never saw the twist coming. When the movie first came out, fans had waited three years for this sequel only to leave theaters in complete shock. No one could have guessed this plot twist that was years in the making, no one except the writer and creator of the Star Wars movies. For George Lucas, the most radical plot twist in movie history was the plan all along.

Plot twists make stories memorable and enjoyable, unless you happen to be the one living through them. Then these unexpected developments are world wreckers, dream killers, your greatest fears coming true in real time.

They are also inevitable. Plot twists are God's way of overriding the story you thought you were writing so it matches the one he already finished. We experience the benefit of a plot twist when we choose not to resist it. It's not proof you're off course; it's confirmation that the journey is bigger, deeper, and more transformative than you imagined.

The road to your dream is never linear. Life throws out unexpected developments and radical changes of direction, both good and bad. The good we don't mind. Rather than call them plot twists, we usually chalk them up to divine blessing or good luck or the result of years of hard work and sacrifice. Whatever we call them, we welcome them, and the more the merrier. Record deals and promotions and financial windfalls don't usually cause crises of faith. Perhaps the hardest part of dealing with them is jaw pain from smiling too much.

There's usually not a lot of smiling when an undesired plot twist hits. Whether detours or delays or betrayals or breakdowns or failures, they test our faith and confidence. The most devastating twists knock us to the ground, leaving us muttering, "Why me?" and, "What now?" The bigger the plot twist, the more damage it inflicts, the more it leaves us questioning everything: our decisions that brought us here, the people we trusted, even the goodness of God. Many a person has crossed over from faith to refusal to believe in God at all not because they doubt he exists but because they cannot believe he would let this twist happen, much less orchestrate it.

**DONOVAN**

And that's the real sticking point. Plot twists take us by surprise, but they do not surprise the author and finisher of our faith (Heb. 12:2). When my dad did not show up in my life, God wasn't caught off guard. He knew what was going to happen and he already knew different men were going to come into my life to fill that father role when I needed it. That is why I can put my trust in him, because he is the writer and director of my life, and he has a plan. All of this is easy to write as I look back, but that doesn't mean it was easy to live through. Yet even the struggle is part of the Director's plan. He promises in Romans 8:28, "And we know that for those who love God all things work together for good, for those who are called according to his purpose" (ESV). He never says all things are going to be good or pleasant or easy to live through. God never promises a life free of plot twists. What he does say is that all of these twists and turns will work together for our good when we hold on and trust him through them, no matter how we found ourselves in them.

### 1. Plot Twists Are Divine Disruptions, Not Accidents

Right now many of you have a problem with this statement. How can we possibly say that plot twists are divine disruptions, not accidents? Does this mean that God wrote bankruptcy into your story? Seriously, that's God's plan? Being stabbed in the back by the partner you trusted, who then stole your dream and left you with nothing but regret? God chose to put that little "divine disruption" in your life? An absent father? Really, that's God's plan? Or divorce, or a miscarriage, or a breakup you never saw coming, or any of a thousand other bad things—are we saying that God thought, "Hey, this guy's life is going too smoothly. Let's throw this curve at him just for fun"?

That is exactly what we are *not* saying. The reality is that we live in a fallen world where worst-case scenarios hit everyone at one time or another. In a world with a death rate of 100 percent, we know no one gets through life unscathed; it's a consequence of sin, whether you believe in God or not. It is too easy to see the whole thing as unfair when you look at it purely from the perspective of self. But when you pull back and see it from the Director's perspective, what you see is not fairness but grace. It is within the arena of his grace that God—the author and completer of our faith—steps in to preserve the narrative he has written for our lives. When things don't go according to plan, that's usually when God is revealing the depth of his authorship. Some of the most powerful moments of life come not from what we planned but from what we are willing to trust in the middle of the twist. To see it, we need to step back from the moment and see what God is doing.

One of the greatest examples of God's divine disruption is found in the story of the exodus of the children of Israel out of Egypt. For four hundred years they had suffered in slavery. Then God crushed Egypt under the weight of ten plagues and set his people free under Moses' leadership. When the Israelites marched out of Egypt, they had their sights set on a land that flowed with milk and honey. They even had a physical manifestation of the presence of God leading them there in the form of a pillar of cloud by day and a pillar of fire by night. But then that pillar of fire led them straight to the shoreline of the Red Sea, with Pharoah's army closing in behind them. When it looked as though their only choices were death by sword or death by drowning, panic set in. The people yelled at Moses, "Didn't we say to you in Egypt, 'Leave us alone; let us serve the Egyptians'? It would have been better for us to serve the Egyptians than to die in the desert!" (Ex. 14:11–12). He tried to calm them down, but they wouldn't listen. The mob was ready to surrender and return to slavery, until God had Moses lift up his staff and the Red Sea split open.

When we recognize plot twists as God's divine disruptions, he shatters our illusion of control over our situation to remind us of Proverbs 19:21: "Many are the plans in a person's heart, but it is the Lord's purpose that prevails." Or as the old saying goes, we plan and God laughs. The goal is to learn to laugh with him and to ask, "What is God doing? What is he trying to teach me?" instead of wailing, "Why me?" Plot twists confront our being, revealing who we are when things do not go as planned. His winding path shows us more and more about ourselves and is intended to deepen the alignment of our identity in him, not in what we do in our own strength to control the outcome. True self-awareness is forged in divine unpredictability. Your faith is measured not just by what you believe at the beginning but by what you hold on to when the plot changes. When you redefine disruption as divine redirection, you shift from fear to formation, which is where soul-safe success begins.

To see how this has played out in your own life, we suggest writing out a chart of your life story, not only what has happened but also what you had planned. Highlight the divergencies, delays, detours, dead ends, and every other unexpected development. How did the twists lead to deeper growth?

## 2. Character Is Forged in the Twist

KEVIN

When Pentatonix won *The Sing-Off*, we also received a recording contract from one of Sony's labels along with a $200,000 advance. For a group of nineteen- to twenty-three-year-olds, we felt like we had reached the pinnacle of our dreams. Winning the show validated our talent, and the record deal gave us instant credibility. We were ecstatic.

Enter the plot twist. The record-label CEO who made our deal left the company. When the new guy came in, he knew nothing about the contract sitting on his desk. As I understood it, all the new CEO saw was a company in critical need of a shot of energy to get it back on top. He already had a stable of established artists with proven track records of success. There weren't any a cappella groups on that list because no a cappella group anywhere had yet achieved the kind of mainstream success that moved the needle. The new CEO had no reason to believe we would be the first.

Eventually our label's new CEO brought us in for a meeting with him and his team. They made us feel right at home and gave us every reason to believe we were now part of the greatest place in the music industry. They showered us with the typical amenities and support every new artist receives. But then came the sit-down meeting with the man who held our future in his hands. We talked about our plans for our first album and touring and all the other things that go into creating a hit record. Somewhere in the middle of the meeting, he asked whether we planned to incorporate instruments into our music. Did we plan on remaining an a cappella group, or would we become a real band backed up by musicians like every other successful group? When we told him that we had no such plans because, by definition, a cappella means without instruments, the CEO sighed and said something about how hard it is to sell that kind of music to the mainstream. Sure, there are fans out there, and he was sure we could have many. But those fans were a niche market, not the kind needed for a hit record.

Of course, we disagreed. We reassured him that we believed we had hit on the right formula to cross over to the mainstream. Also, we had our existing fans from *The Sing-Off* to consider. We were building up a base that we did not want to abandon just to chase a possibility. The CEO said he completely understood, and the meeting ended on good terms. A few weeks later the label let our manager know that they felt they lacked the expertise to assist us. They were not the right fit for us. They wished us well and offered a contract kill fee to make their problem go away.

And that was that. We were still winners of a television talent show that stayed on the air for only eight more episodes after our win, and that was it. No label. No record deal. We were back at square one. The future we thought had already arrived was now gone, and we had no idea what to do next.

Looking back, I do not know whether Pentatonix would have attained the success we enjoy today if that exec had not canceled our first record deal. In the aftermath, we had to be more creative in our pursuits, leading us to make interesting choices in covers and medleys, such as "Evolution of Music" (a medley of songs from Gregorian chants to modern-day hits) or our "Daft Punk Medley." It forced us to create more innovative music that would captivate listeners and viewers on YouTube. We also learned to operate almost like independent artists, even when we eventually did sign with a major label. No one can do our work for us like we can. A label can't guarantee our success. A label is our partner, providing suggestions, securing promo and press opportunities, and assisting with sync placements. But at the end of the day, the thing that drives our success is the great music we create that resonates with our fans and attracts new ones. This makes the label's job much easier in terms of promotion. The plot twist we encountered was a significant turning point in our journey. Our character as a band grew out of the absolute worst-case scenario coming true.

That experience also changed me. At first I was quite shaken. I had given up my dream of going to medical school for the band, and suddenly that looked like the worst decision of a lifetime. "God, is this a joke?" I prayed. "Did you really bring me here to fail?" But then I went back to the day of my junior year of college when I believed that God had revealed that his plan for my life was music. I faced a choice now. Would I trust him and keep following or figure out my own plan B? It was easy to say I believed God in my dorm library, but now the stakes were much higher. My faith had to be bigger and my trust stronger. In this plot twist, and the many that followed, I learned how God is less interested in my dream than he is in making me into the kind of person who can carry his dream with character.

James 1:2 challenges us to consider the unexpected developments and radical changes of direction as opportunities for great joy. To do so requires a complete mind shift, which James goes on to explain: "For you know that when your faith is tested, your endurance has a chance to grow. So let it grow, for when your endurance is fully developed, you will be perfect and complete, needing nothing" (vv. 3–4 NLT). Troubles and trials prepare you for impact. The person you become through hardship has more integrity, empathy, tenacity, and power than you could ever have apart from it. These setbacks are actually the preparation ground for the future that God has called you to occupy. But to see it you have to look beyond the moment to what God is doing as a whole.

To see how this is playing out in your life, we suggest you map out your past failures and disappointments:

- Trace how many became the foundations for new chapters God is writing in your life.

- Journal what God is doing now, even if it is messy. Especially if it is messy. Revisit in six months. What has changed? How have you changed? What new dreams or visions or projects or successes rose out of the ashes of disappointment?
- Finally, share what you've discovered with a friend who is navigating the confusion of plot twists in their own life, not to brag but to encourage.

### 3. Let Go of the Plan and Hold On to the Purpose

DONOVAN

I had a plan. A big one. I sold my home, giving up the stability and comfort that came with it, and chose temporarily to rent rooms in people's houses while my grand plan came together. I used the proceeds to do three things straight from my heart.

I invested heavily into the equipment and promotion of my entrepreneurial endeavors as a life coach, photographer, and author.

I invested in other entrepreneurs and small-business owners in whose visions I believed.

I gave generously to people I saw in need, whether it was to fund the cost of a mission trip or pay a bill to keep them afloat.

The moves felt good. They felt purposeful. They felt exactly like the kind of bold, faith-filled moves someone living out their calling would make. None of them felt risky. Selling my house for these pursuits seemed like a momentary sacrifice that would pay off quickly.

But there was one small catch in my big plans. I based them on my feelings and assumed that God approved. I never actually stopped to ask. I followed my heart, but I never paused and submitted my plan to God. I asked him to bless it, but I never asked whether he wanted this for me in this particular season.

Once I set my plan into motion, I expected to see results. I expected my coaching business to explode through television and radio interviews, panel discussions, workshops and conferences, book partnerships, and consulting. I saw myself living off the return while I kept investing in other people and giving generously. But my plan didn't go as planned. My business grew moderately in impact, but not financially, at least not enough to meet my basic needs. I was the one who was now struggling to stay afloat. My rent was past due, my truck was almost repossessed, my self-care routine was no longer sustainable, my heart was confused, and my soul was vexed. I burned through the money I made on my house much faster than I thought possible without seeing a return. Suddenly I was staring at bills I couldn't pay.

The more the bills piled up, the more I prayed. I quoted Proverbs 11:25 back to God. "You promised the generous will prosper and those who refresh others will themselves be refreshed," I said to him. I tried not to think about how Jesus said we should store up treasure in heaven, which is what generosity in his name does. That's hard to think about when we need a withdrawal from that treasure to keep the lights on down here on earth.

I finally reached a point where I needed to consider doing something I had resisted all my adult life. It was time to go the nine-to-five route in corporate America. I'd always told myself I would never do that again. It wasn't me. It wasn't freedom. And it sure wasn't the dream I'd sold my house to chase. But when you are standing at the edge of the canyon between the life you expected and the life you have, you do what has to be done. I realized that idolizing the pursuit of the things I was passionate about was my biggest downfall. Even our passions must be submitted to purpose and divine design. Through the process, I discovered that God had shifted not only my direction but also my understanding of what was good for me.

God basically dragged me into a nine-to-five job kicking and screaming through the guidance of my most trusted mentor, who referred me to a particular company because he knew my integrity and saw my potential. He recommended me to a person in upper management who created a unique role for me after I interviewed. Even with that I still fought within myself not to see taking this job as a failure. Every Sabbath I reminded myself that God cannot lie, he will do as he promises, and he has a plan to prosper me, not to harm me. These confessions refreshed my soul and defeated the doubt that so stubbornly wanted to lead me down an emotional road of depression and self-pity.

God delivered.

My new job brought stability when I needed it the most. It gave me access to market resources, professional relationships, and skills that became the foundation of my coaching business. I was allowed to enroll in certification programs at the company's expense that expanded my knowledge. I sat with clinical therapists and gleaned from their years of mastery, refining and customizing my signature approach to connecting with and coaching clients through a mental health lens. I was even asked to do in-services, opportunities to group coach my coworkers, which aided in the development of my leadership expertise. What I thought was an unnecessary detour turned out to be the ground floor of the platform God was building for me. The detours helped develop the dream so that it could live outside of myself through purpose.

Too often we confuse purpose and dream as one and the same. They're not. Our dreams may take on many forms in different seasons in life, but our purpose does not change. It is rooted in our identity. Surrendering a dream is not giving up. Rather, surrender makes space for divine alignment. We treat interruptions as violations of our vision, when in reality they're divine invitations to level up our identity. The plot twist isn't the end of your dream but the bridge to the version of you that can live out your purpose without compromising your soul.

I thought my dream was to coach full time. If I could do life coaching full time, that had to mean I was really good at what I was doing. That's the measure I needed to give me validation. I lost sight of the fact that life coaching is my calling that grows out of my purpose of glorifying God by investing my life in others to help them find purpose and meaning in their own lives in him. Whether I do this for forty or fifty hours a week or in my free time after my nine-to-five job does not matter to God. All that matters is that I align myself with him and live out his purpose.

Surrendering often feels difficult. Remember, you don't have to understand the plot unfolding in your life to trust the

Author. Keep turning the page. The story isn't over and neither is your dream. Reflect on a current or past plot twist you've lived through. What would your future self say to you right now? If this is a hard truth for you, we invite you to offer up this prayer of surrender: "God, I release what I expected and receive what you intended." God's detours often lead to better destinations than we ever could have mapped out ourselves. As you pray, allow the following to guide your conversation:

- What plot twist in your life shook you the most? Why?
- What were you forced to let go of that you thought was essential? What made letting go so difficult? What happened when you finally released it?
- As you reflect on the plot twists you've lived through, what have you gained through them that you could not have gained any other way?
- What is one area of your life where you are resisting the plot twist? Offer up a letter of surrender.

CHAPTER 12

# LET GOD DO THE GOD STUFF

DONOVAN

When I first stepped into the life-coaching arena, I thought I knew how to make it work. Everything I read said to start with a strong social media presence, then invest in paid ads, maybe even secure an agent or PR firm. I attempted most of it. I posted motivational videos, wrote carefully curated captions, sought referrals for podcast and radio interviews. But the truth? My inbox didn't fill up, my calendar didn't fill up, and my spirit felt—off. I really had no idea what to do next.

During one of my Sabbath breaks, God impressed something on my heart that shifted my entire approach: "Start with serving, not seeking profit." I'd never heard anything like this in a business podcast or from a sales coach. It felt very counterintuitive. You start a business to make a profit; otherwise, you don't stay in business very long. But the longer I remained in this state of prayer and stillness before God, the more certain I was that this was directly from him. How could I tell? Because it sounded exactly like what the one who washed his disciples' feet would say. It echoed Jesus' words when he said, "For even the Son of Man did not come to be served, but to serve" (Mark 10:45). I realized I'd been trying to do God's job by forcing growth instead of doing my job by simply being faithful with the gifts I had.

"Start with serving, not seeking profit" called for a complete change of strategy. Instead of doubling my efforts to find paying clients, I started a monthly free event I called "Coach-Shop" that blended the heart of group coaching with the practical tools of a workshop. No ticket price, no funnel, no hidden upsell. Just a space where people could experience transformation without worrying about what they could afford. The Coach-Shop was my firstfruit type of offering to God, the Old Testament idea to give the first part of the harvest as an offering to God rather than part of whatever was left over at the end (Ex. 23:19). Pouring my time, skill, and energy into these free events was my way of saying, with a heart driven by gratitude instead of worry, "God, this isn't mine. It's yours. I'm just the steward." The reward would come through the impact Coach-Shop made in the lives of those who attended.

If anyone attended.

When I opened the door for my first Coach-Shop, I was nervous. I did not have an RSVP list. In all my promotions I'd encouraged people to just show up. When the first few people arrived, I felt a sense of confirmation that this really was a God thing. With time I realized that attendance numbers aren't an indication of anything except that people showed up. The real confirmation comes as the Holy Spirit prompts you and brings to mind Scripture verses that settle you into a place of assurance and peace. Even though I was sure that God was in this approach, part of me still questioned why I was giving away for free what I had already invested a great deal of time and money in. Then God reminded me that he is my source. As Jesus said in the Sermon on the Mount, seek first his kingdom and God will take care of the rest. I believe he meant what he said. And then came a powerful mantra I still commonly use today: I never run out of good ideas. I don't have to be selfish with what God has given me or keep all the ideas to myself, because *he* is the unlimited source. I can share without fear of running out of clever ideas or solutions or innovations because this is a generosity built on trust in the one who gives me every good and profitable idea that I have ever needed and ever will need; it's simply part of how he designed me. He spoke to my heart that he'd always intended to do it this way. I decided to walk by faith instead of walking in fear that my ideas would be plagiarized or that my big break was dependent on making sure I got credit for something God gave me to share.

Here's the wild thing: Without any pitching from me, a few people offered to pay for private coaching. With time, almost every person who attended a Coach-Shop became a one-on-one client. Many of the people who attended those free sessions also began referring friends, family, and colleagues to me. They were even offering to pay for the first sessions for the person they referred. That's how much they wanted people to experience this coaching. This wasn't hustle. This was harvest—God's harvest. One attendee worked at a hospital, which then contacted me and offered a leadership-coaching contract to coach its staff of doctors and nurses. More doors opened up with invitations to speak on panels at other workshops, along with radio interviews. All the doors that had once seemed locked or had slammed in my face opened up when I began to serve without seeking profit.

Looking back, I now understand how that year of my doing free Coach-Shops embodied the heart of "Let God do the God stuff":

- My part: Show up, obey the prompting, give my best without strings attached
- God's part: Open the right doors, stir the right hearts, bring the right opportunities
- Result: A business that wasn't just built but blessed

When you honor God first, you won't have to chase what he's already assigned to you. My job was obedience. His job was outcome. When we stop trying to be God and simply walk with him, we realize he's far better at his job than we are. If we're designed to succeed, then the whole process starts with understanding the difference between what is ours to do and what God will handle, trusting in God's timing and practicing a strategy of submission to God's will.

### 1. Know the Line Between Your Stuff and God's Stuff

DONOVAN

If I could go back to when I was trying to figure out how to market myself and work through all the emotions of unmet expectations, I would simply ask myself, "If God called you to this, what role do you believe he plans to play in the success of it?" This is the essential and most difficult question we must ask when seeking to place ourselves on a trajectory of success. Most driven people (which, since you have made it this far in a book about success, most likely includes you) believe we are the key to our own success. No one is going to hand us anything, which means we have to work and push and grind to make it happen. God's role is to bless our efforts. He pours gasoline on the fire we started to achieve our dreams on our timetable for our benefit. He is also welcome to step in and handle any huge, unforeseen emergencies. Beyond that, we can handle it. But that approach is completely wrong. It reduces God and inflates us. It's backward.

Proverbs 3:5–6 says, "Trust in the Lord with all your heart and lean not on your own understanding; in all your ways submit to him, and he will make your paths straight." The passage has three commands that directly influence our pursuit of success: Trust. Lean not. Submit. These build to a promise. The Lord will make your path straight. Implied in this passage is another command: Follow. Follow God's path, not your own. Let God do the God stuff. Why? He is wiser than we are. He sees the beginning, middle, and end of this journey while we can see only what is directly in front of us. He has the power to accomplish his plan, while we do not. He is never confused, never tempted, never pulled off course by something shiny. He's not like us.

More than that is the truth that God is the source of our identity, the sustainer of our purpose, and the designer of our destiny. He is the why, when, and how of our lives. Anything that falls within that territory is the God stuff. In response, our role is to align ourselves with what he says is true about us. We make ourselves available to be used when and how he sees fit, letting him set the agenda. This doesn't mean being passively indifferent or giving up. Instead we are allowing the benefit of a partnership with heaven to wash over us. When we let God do the God stuff, we are free to steward the gifts he entrusts to us and experiment, perfect, practice, and create. Anchored in trust, obedience, and identity, we don't have to force the results. We can leave them to him.

So how do we know whether we have blurred the line between God's role and our own? Here are some clear signs:

- We're exhausted from ignoring the essentials.
- We're impatient with timelines.
- We wrestle with bouts of anxiety.
- We struggle with fearful thoughts.
- We panic on a regular basis.

When we stay on our side and allow God to do what only he can, there is a very different outcome:

- We have constant peace even when the future is unclear.
- We don't obsess over details.

- Our faithfulness feels simple and unforced.
- We celebrate more often.
- We see people drawn not just to our gifts but to how grounded we are.
- We experience doors being opened by people who simply feel compelled to open them.

## 2. Trust God's Timing More Than Your Timeline

KEVIN

With God, timing is more important than time. This has always been God's design. Galatians 4:4 says, "But when the set time had fully come, God sent his Son, born of a woman, born under the law." Think about it: Jesus could have come earlier or later, but the Lord knew when the timing was right for him to arrive. There was a ripening of a situation and circumstance that God allowed and created—Roman dominion over the Jews, the Jewish leaders in cahoots with Rome, and the Jews' desire for liberation from the Romans—that made Jesus' message ripe for people to receive. The time was also ripe for the Jewish leaders to oppose him and ultimately kill him. But that wasn't the end of God's plan. On the third day, Jesus rose and sent his followers out into the world. Thanks to Roman rule, roads stretched far and wide across the empire, along with trade routes across the Mediterranean, which allowed the good news about Jesus to spread across the known world. Only the Lord's sovereign wisdom and timing could make that happen.

When you trust God's pace and timing, you step into the masterpiece he's crafting in your own life. I've seen this as a cellist who's played in orchestras. I know the conductor sees the entire score and knows when each instrument is supposed to come in. He sets the tempo for the whole orchestra to move at his pace, because he understands the emotion he's trying to make his audience feel. Similarly, God is the universe's great conductor who sets the tempo and aligns people and situations based on his ordained schedule. He sees the entire picture and understands what will benefit his plan—and *you* are a part of that overarching plan. This means that things may not unfold as quickly as you desire or in the manner you anticipate. You may feel like you're walking blind, but this is where you'll need to trust that the Maker can put everything in place.

This is why, even as we plan our course, we must trust that God establishes every step according to his will and in his timing, taking into account the best interests of all parties involved.

Throughout my life, I have been amazed at God's timing. I had a front-row seat to it when God brought two opportunities my way after I graduated from college: touring with the band Gungor and joining Pentatonix. I should not have been able to do both, but God wove events together so that I could. His timing was impeccable. As I watched his hand at work, I was amazed every step of the way. It was like a master class in divine timing.

Trusting in God's timing more than our own timeline is easy when he fast-tracks events for our good. The real challenge, though, comes when God's pace feels like glacial creep. Then we find ourselves frustrated more than amazed, which soon turns into the temptation to take things into our own hands. I certainly understood that temptation in 2019. Some brokers with whom

I had worked for a very long time told me about an investment property in Kentucky. It included restaurant space, as well as a small office unit. Everything in the deal looked great: good property, good location. More important, I trusted the brokers because they had done a few investment-property deals for me in the past. So I told them, "Let's do this and get this deal wrapped up." I figured everything would be simple going forward, since that's how past deals had gone. Boy, was I wrong.

I won't bore you with all the details, but whatever could go wrong did. From legal questions to an issue with a grease trap in the restaurant to disputes with the group managing the condominiums above us, every time I thought the deal was going to go through, another delay popped up. So many times I thought, *This deal isn't worth it. Maybe I should move on.* What made it even more frustrating was that this was just an investment for me, a way to diversify and set up some long-term financial plans for later, after life in a band. Buying real estate was not some kind of artistic expression; it was simply a way to plant some of the fruit I'd received and hopefully see it increase over time. One thing everyone in the entertainment industry knows is that most artists have a short shelf life. There is no guarantee that the sold-out tours and platinum albums of today will continue into tomorrow, which is why my father told me, "You should always be planting seeds with your money." Invest today for an uncertain tomorrow. That's all I was trying to do with this Kentucky property. But instead I kept slamming my head into the wall of delay, delay, delay.

Looking back, I can see that the delays were actually God's

perfect timing. I thought the deal would be wrapped up by spring 2019, but it stretched into the fall and nearly to winter. In the meantime, I got married in September, which meant my wife was now an equal partner in my investments, as well as an equal beneficiary. Since the two of us had gone from two separate individuals to one flesh, I wanted every part of our lives to be intertwined. At the end of 2019, the deal finally came together. Less than three months later, in March 2020, I was sitting at home with very little to do. Pentatonix's tour had shut down and none of us knew when, or even if, we might get to tour again. No touring meant no touring income. One of the only income streams I had through the pandemic was—you guessed it—a restaurant in Kentucky I just happened to now own. What had felt like endless delays turned out to be perfect timing after all.

There is an uncomfortable question we all have to ask ourselves: "What part of my dream or my life am I afraid to release because I don't trust God's timing?" We can discover exactly where we're not trusting through these tells:

- When I complain about delays, I don't trust God's timing.
- When I obsess over the schedule for my dream and get stressed when I fall behind, I don't trust God's timing.
- When I have to control every part of everything I'm doing and I become angry over any disruption, I don't trust God's timing.
- When I become impatient and my tolerance for simple mistakes is at an all-time low, I don't trust God's timing.

- When my prayers are more driven by requests than grounded in gratitude, I don't trust God's timing.
- When I find it hard to be kind to others, I don't trust God's timing.

Whether it's a real-estate deal or a dream you believe in, you'll find that trusting God's timing comes down to surrendering control over your schedule. It requires laying your timelines and charts and graphs at his feet and saying, "Your timing, Lord. Not mine."

### 3. Let God Take Charge, and Submit to His Plan

DONOVAN

The night before Jesus went to the cross, he prayed, "My Father, if it is possible, may this cup be taken from me. Yet not as I will, but as you will" (Matt. 26:39). Jesus was in agony. He was about to take the sin of all the world onto himself and pay the penalty for it for all time. The physical pain ahead of him paled in comparison with the anguish of being separated from his Father while he hung on the cross. He pleaded with his Father to find some other way of reconciling the human race back to him. But in the end he prayed, "Not as I will, but as you will." Whatever you want me to do, I'll do it. No matter what. This is the perfect example of what submission to the will and plan of our Creator looks like. It is telling the Father, "Whatever you want, God, that's what I want." This is the confession that lets God do the God stuff. As Bono very wisely said, "Don't ask God to bless what you're doing. Get involved in what God is doing—because it's already blessed." Give him permission to take over your life. And yes, letting God take charge and submitting to him applies to every aspect of our lives, even when it turns our plans upside down.

I discovered this truth shortly after making the final payment on my luxury SUV. I was finally finished with my monthly payments and interest. My truck was all mine! I felt a great sense of liberation made even sweeter because this was the same truck that had almost gotten repossessed a few seasons earlier. Now with the truck paid off I could finally enjoy life and take hold of new opportunities that hadn't been available before. I was so grateful as I basked in the moment; I felt like I was walking into the promised land. My mind also went into strategy mode: How much I could save now, how quickly I could hit my investment targets, how soon I could partner in a real-estate deal I'd been eyeing, how much I could spend on new self-care routines and places I wanted to travel.

Then that December, during one of my quiet morning prayer times, I felt that unmistakable nudge from the Holy Spirit: *Give the truck to him.* I didn't know who "him" was at first. Then I clearly pictured him in my mind as though on a projection screen. *Him?* I thought. *The man I've met only a few times? The man who hasn't even asked for it?*

My flesh wanted to fight. My logic wanted to audit the command. I pleaded with God, "No, not another plot twist, not another sacrifice on the mountain, not another trial-by-fire moment." I could list ten "better" uses for that truck in five seconds flat. But here's the thing: When you're truly submitted to

God, you've given him veto power over your plans, even the smart or seemingly responsible ones. The Holy Spirit's role in our lives is not to rubber-stamp our dreams but to guide us into God's plans and design for us. Sometimes that guidance comes in the form of radical generosity that makes zero financial or business sense. And that's where submission becomes the bridge between a personally satisfying moment and an entirely blessed life.

When the Spirit nudged me to give away my paid-in-full SUV, I had to confront a subtle idol I didn't even know I had: my need for everything to make sense. I realized I had started worshiping clarity instead of trusting the creator of the mystery. If left unchecked, our imagination can paralyze us with fear when we think about living an open-handed walk of faith. That may have been what I was experiencing. But what I had to understand was that God doesn't owe us an explanation before he asks for our obedience. He simply asks us to trust that he always has our best interests at heart. Did I believe that? I always said I did. But did I believe it enough to do something that felt completely backward and unwise, something that did not make sense in my mind, something that turned over all the plans I had made for myself?

Jesus said, "Store up for yourselves treasures in heaven, where moths and vermin do not destroy, and where thieves do not break in and steal" (Matt. 6:20). Well, so the story goes, on Christmas Day, December 25, 2022, I handed the keys and the title of my truck to the one God had chosen. I didn't do it for a big thank-you. I didn't want the man to feel like he was indebted to me because of this gift. I didn't even record the exchange and post it on social media as I had done with other events and celebrations I attended. This was a gift, and a gift, by definition, is given with no thought or expectation of anything in return. Instead, I learned that in giving away my SUV, I wasn't losing an asset. I was making a deposit in an eternal bank account.

I don't know what the Holy Spirit may ask you to do. No one does except God himself. The question we all face is this: When God's instruction disrupts your plan, will you cling to your strategy, or trust the one who authored the perfect story for your planned success? This obedience is the essence of letting God be God. When your ego subsides, you will see how beautifully positioned you are for fulfillment, for freedom, for unexpected gifts that you never could have imagined on your own.

CHAPTER 13

# NEVER STOP LEARNING

KEVIN

In 2024 my high-performance coach, Brian, posed a profound question that I found very difficult to answer. He asked me, "If God asked you to leave the band, would you?" I hesitated. After all the Grammys, platinum albums, and financial success I'd experienced as a part of Pentatonix, why would I ever think about walking away? In addition to the financial certainty, being a part of the band also gave me a cachet that opens doors and the ability to provide a certain lifestyle for my family.

It also gave me a false sense of self-worth based on my achievements.

Brian must have read my mind because he added, "Even if you were given one hundred million dollars to leave the band, would you?"

For any sane person, this wouldn't even be a question. Probably everyone reading this book would jump at the offer. But I hesitated. I don't know why. Maybe it is because I've devoted my entire adult life to this one job and I don't know what I'd do with my time without it. I'm also very comfortable as one of five. Over the past decade and a half, we've developed a routine for our work. The five of us know one another so well and work with and off one another so effectively that I'm not certain I could do anything else independently at this juncture. But then there's a bigger question: What if whatever I do after Pentatonix doesn't succeed? What would my friends, family, neighbors say? "Well, Kevin, you should've just stayed where you were already successful."

On top of everything else, no matter how hard I try otherwise, a huge part of my identity is wrapped up in what I do. I know I am more than my work. I am a husband and a father and, more than anything else, a child of God. But professionally, who would I be? What's my identity to myself? I finally stopped thinking and started talking. I tried to share everything with my coach, but I was stuttering the whole time. I couldn't really be this raw with all of these thoughts, could I?

But he could tell I wasn't being forthcoming. "Do you know why you're hesitating?" he asked.

I didn't answer.

"You think being in the band is your safety net. You're not realizing that it's God who gave you all of these things and put you in this position. You didn't earn any of this. So don't you realize that you need to have faith enough to know that if God called you out, he would provide all your needs for his purpose in your life?"

I now understand that in that moment I was very much like the wealthy young man to whom Jesus said, "Sell all your possessions and follow me." The reason why walking away from everything was exceptionally challenging for me is the same reason it was difficult for this young man. To even entertain the idea that God could call me away from Pentatonix demands my complete surrender of my entire life—even its most challenging aspects—to him.

That's the danger of falling for the myth of arrival in the success journey. When you think your journey has come to an end, you stop learning to prepare for tomorrow. Then when tomorrow arrives, and it always arrives, you find yourself lost. You think God has let you down or pulled the rug out from under you instead of understanding that his purpose for you is now going to play out in a new arena. In life, change is the only constant. Nothing remains the same.

Today I am the father of two young children. One day I will turn around and they will be teenagers with a completely different set of challenges for me as their father. The next day, they will be grown and out of the house, which, I have been told, is the most difficult stage of being a parent.

I have not arrived yet. The journey is never over. The same is especially true of my professional life. With very few exceptions, every band has a lifespan. Popularity rises and falls; members come and go. The day may well come when Pentatonix no longer exists. Will I be ready?

Every stage of success in every part of life requires a deeper level of surrender and refinement. The moment you crown yourself your own teacher is the moment you stop being teachable and step out of God's design for your success. And so the question we must continually ask ourselves is not "Am I done?" but "Am I still willing to grow?"

## God Is Still Teaching You Because He's Still Growing You

DONOVAN

I remember being invited to a personal-development seminar. I was a little unsure about going because I wasn't familiar with the organization. But I did what any responsible adult would do and asked someone more in the know about it. The person I asked was my mentor, who also happened to be the master coach who trained me. He told me that he was familiar with the organization and that I was grounded enough in my faith to be able to reap the core benefit of what they had to offer without being swept away by the nuances.

On the first day, I walked into the seminar and saw all the chairs, the whiteboards, the projection screen, the coffee and pastries, and of course my fellow attendees. Some looked eager, some skeptical, and a few even looked as though they'd rather be anywhere but there. I was somewhere in the middle. Part of me was open, but part of me was on guard. I wanted to flow and engage with a student mindset, but I also had some trust issues from previous experiences. This wasn't my first workshop or course like this. I was in the middle of training to become a life coach and had already started forming a lot of my opinions about what works and what doesn't. I was cautiously optimistic that I might pick up something useful over the next few days.

It didn't take long for me to go from skeptical to all in.

During one of the early sessions, one of the facilitators dropped a line that caught me completely off guard: "The moment you think you have it all figured out is the moment your growth stops." It was like she was speaking directly to me. *The moment you think you have made it is the moment your growth stops.* Guilty as charged. Whether it was booking a big speaking gig or gaining recognition or hitting a milestone, I secretly assumed that every one of these moments was a finish line, and I lusted for them as if they were the answers to every problem in my life. I now had to face an uncomfortable truth. Success is not a ladder you climb and then sit at the top of enjoying the view. Instead, it is more like a beautiful endless spiral staircase. Every step up gives you a new vantage point while also revealing another turn ahead.

These thoughts stayed with me long after the workshop was over. I took a fresh look at the finish lines I'd crossed. I saw now that each one was a place where God had planted seeds for rooms I had not yet entered. I am not a finished product. None of us are. We are to always remain in the process of becoming by aligning. That is where God meets us. Romans 12:2 tells us, "Do not conform to the pattern of this world, but be transformed by the renewing of your mind." The word *renewing* refers to a continuous process. Like water, a mind stagnates when nothing new flows in and nothing old flows out. But it is renewed when we learn and question and explore. Proverbs 9:9 says, "Give instruction to a wise man, and he will be still wiser; teach a righteous man, and he will increase in learning" (ESV). That is God's divine design for us, a lifetime of ever increasing wisdom that continues as long as we resist the arrogance of "I've arrived" and stay present to the work he is doing in us right now. Philippians 1:6 says, "Being confident of this, that he who began a good work in you will carry it on to completion until the day of Christ Jesus." God's design for you isn't a snapshot. It's a living, breathing masterpiece.

To the cynics who say, "People don't change," I'd reply, "No, they evolve if they choose to." But evolution requires humility and surrender. It demands that you step into each day as both a student of and a participant in God's ongoing creation. You'll always have an opportunity to learn because God never stops teaching. Every challenge is a curriculum that can help you cultivate your character and realize your potential. Every victory is a practicum than can refine your vision and your intention. And every person God sends your way is either a teacher or a student, sometimes both. St. Augustine is thought to have said, "The world is a book, and those who do not travel read only one page."

Keep turning the pages. Your story—and your growth—is not finished.

## Three Practical Steps to Keep a Student's Heart

There is a difference between knowing the path and walking it. Here are three steps that we've learned keep us at the feet of the Master, where we get to soak up all we can from him:

1. *Schedule weekly check-ins with the Holy Spirit.* Don't wait until you feel burned out or hit a wall. At regular intervals each week, spend time alone with God and whisper the prayer, "What are you trying to teach me, Lord?" Go back to chapter 11 on plot twists and chapter 12 on letting God do the God stuff. Recognize that setbacks and delays can be the most trying times to keep our ears attuned to God's lessons.
2. *Surround yourself with voices that challenge and sharpen you.* When God teaches, he often uses a human voice. Find coaches, mentors, pastors, or peers who are wise but who also love you enough to call out your blind spots. Many of the lessons we most need to learn are ones we don't even realize we need. Proverbs 27:17 says, "As iron sharpens iron, so one person sharpens another." Sharpening comes with friction. Be open to learning from those who are so different from you that you prefer to avoid them. What might God be saying to you through them?
3. *Practice the daily pause of humility.* In James 1:5, God promises to give wisdom to anyone who asks. Before making key decisions or forming conclusions, ask, "What do I still need to learn about this?" One of the greatest signs of wisdom is the humility to admit what you do not know and the willingness to learn more.

Remember, if you are still alive, you have yet to graduate from God's school. That's the beauty of God's plan. Every challenge is a new course. Every victory is a new degree. As long as you are breathing, you're enrolled. Keep showing up for class. Keep sharpening your mind, your craft, and your character. Heaven's curriculum is customized for each of us. Some lessons will stretch you, others will heal you, and all will shape you. Offer up each new day as a new page in God's syllabus for your life and success. The tests are real, but so are the breakthroughs. Every test is evidence that you are being considered for a promotion. Don't rush the lesson. God's wisdom has no expiration date, and neither does his calling on you. Trust the Teacher. You are not just learning to succeed. You are learning to steward success God's way. After all, that's what he designed you to do.

You've now seen that true success isn't manufactured, it's revealed through alignment with your unique design, developed through intentional growth, and multiplied when fueled by faith. Our formula for success is alignment plus development times faith. Every story, every principle, every shift you've encountered in these pages has been preparing you for what lies ahead. As you step into the future, you'll find that the perspective you've gained here will dramatically improve your confidence when facing tests, your courage when facing challenges, and your discernment when facing new opportunities. This isn't just a book to finish, it's a blueprint to return to alongside your continual study of God's holy Word, a compass to keep in your hands, and a conversation to share with your friends so that accountability strengthens your journey. And above all, never forget the most important book in the world, the Holy Bible, in which you'll find the inspiration for this book and God's own success formula, declared in Joshua 1:8: "Keep this Book of the Law always on your lips; meditate on it day and night, so that you may be careful to do everything written in it. Then you will be prosperous and successful." This is not the end of your story. It's the launch of your destiny.

ACKNOWLEDGMENTS

DONOVAN DEE DONNELL

There are far more people in this book than are named on the cover. Some of them prayed for me. Some of them doubted me. Some of them paid me. Some of them corrected me. Some of them disappointed me. And all of them, in one way or another, helped design the man writing these words.

First, to my mom: You were my first teacher in discernment, strength, and grace. You taught me how to think, how to sit with myself, and how to listen before reacting. You didn't just raise a son, you raised a conscience. Thank you for believing in me long before I had language for who I was becoming, and for loving me through every version of myself, including the confusing ones.

To my grandfather: You introduced me to faith not as performance but as responsibility. You showed me what it looks like to serve people with conviction and compassion, and how to lead without needing applause. You built a spiritual foundation sturdy enough to hold me even when I tried to outrun it. I stand on your shoulders more often than I probably admit.

To my father, who is no longer here: There are things I wish

I said, and things I wish I understood sooner. But your presence, your absence, and your legacy all shaped me. And to every father figure who stepped in along the way, intentionally or accidentally: Thank you for filling gaps, offering guidance, setting boundaries, or simply modeling what manhood can look like in different forms. I needed every version.

To my former exotic dancer friends, brothers in the grind, the hustle, the late nights, and the unspoken questions: You saw me at my most performative and my most conflicted. You taught me about survival, about hunger, about the cost of applause, and about how quickly the lights go out. To the fans, the tippers, the ones who showed up night after night and paid for a version of me that wasn't fully me yet: Thank you. You were part of the journey, even if you never knew the internal war that was happening on the other side of the smile.

To my friends from school, from the neighborhood, from before anyone thought there was a brand or a calling attached to my name: You knew me when success was still just a feeling and not a title. You kept me grounded, checked me when necessary, and reminded me where I came from when it mattered most.

To every person who told me no, every door that closed, every opportunity that passed me by, every rejection that forced me to sit with myself longer than I wanted to: Thank you. You didn't derail my life, you refined it. You made me ask better questions. You slowed me down long enough to discover who I was instead of who I thought I needed to be.

To Kevin Olusola, my brother, my friend, my colaborer in this work: Thank you for trusting me with your story, your faith, your questions, and your voice. This book is richer because of your honesty, your discipline, and your willingness to wrestle out loud.

To Mark Tabb: Thank you for helping us shape this message with clarity and care and for respecting both the weight and the wonder of these stories.

To Kor Element: Thank you for accepting me, for planting the seeds of this vision, lighting fire under the process, and helping bring new eyes to the creative process.

And finally, to God, the patient architect of my becoming: Thank you for not giving up on me when I misunderstood success, when I chased applause, when I tried to wear crowns I wasn't designed to carry. Thank you for designing a life that still feels like it's unfolding and for reminding me that success isn't about becoming someone else but is about returning to who I was created to be.

If this book helps anyone feel a little more aligned, a little more honest, and a little more free, then every step of the journey was worth it.

### KEVIN OLUSOLA

To Pentatonix and my management: You expanded my world beyond what I thought possible. Through discipline, trust, and shared excellence, you taught me lessons that will echo far beyond the stage.

To my mother: You whispered early that ordinary was never my calling and showed me that greatness is cultivated—by faith, by courage, and by choosing the uncommon path.

To my father: Your life testified that adversity does not have the final word and that rising above the odds is an act of quiet faith.

To my siblings, my first team, my lifelong witnesses: Thank you for standing with me in every chapter.

To Donovan, my brother: Your character sharpened mine, your friendship steadied me, your life lessons continue to shape the man I am becoming.

To Kor Element: Your vision reached farther than the present moment, helping us to see not only what was but what could be.

To Mark Tabb: You gave language to thought, structure to story, and meaning to moments that asked to be remembered.

To my wife, the keeper of my heart: You made room for my calling and, through your love, taught me what it means to serve well.

To my children, my greatest joy: I leave these pages to you so you may know not only what your father did but why he did it.

And to Almighty God, who knew me before breath filled my lungs, before purpose took shape, before I could speak his name: All that I am is because of you, and all that I offer is in your service.

# NOTES

1. *New Oxford American Dictionary*, 3rd ed. (2010), under "success."
2. Quoted in T. D. Jakes, "When Men Fall Short—Drawn to Praise—Bishop T. D. Jakes," posted June 22, 2015, by the Potter's House of Dallas, YouTube, 1 hr., 4 min., www.youtube .com/watch?v=ISWQIjNABeE.
3. Quoted in Dave Raffo, "Duane Thomas Reflects on Silent 1971 Season," UPI Archives, October 29, 1988, www.upi.com /Archives/1988/10/29/Duane-Thomas-Reflects-On-Silent-1971 -Season/9261594100800.
4. Marcus E. Raichle, "The Brain's Default Mode Network," *Annual Review of Neuroscience* 38 (July 2015): 433–47, https:// doi.org/10.1146/annurev-neuro-071013-014030; Mary Helen Immordino-Yang, Joanna A. Christodoulou, and Vanessa Singh, "Rest Is Not Idleness: Implications of the Brain's Default Mode for Human Development and Education," *Perspectives on Psychological Science* 7, no. 4 (2012): 352–64, https://doi .org/10.1177/1745691612447308; Srini Pillay, "Secret to Brain Success: Intelligent Cognitive Rest," Harvard Health Publishing, May 4, 2017, www.health.harvard.edu/blog/secret-to-brain -success-intelligent-cognitive-rest-2017050411705.

*From the Publisher*

# GREAT BOOKS

## ARE EVEN BETTER WHEN THEY'RE SHARED!

**Help other readers find this one:**

- Post a review at your favorite online bookseller
- Post a picture on a social media account and share why you enjoyed it
- Send a note to a friend who would also love it—or better yet, give them a copy

*Thanks for reading!*